—DETOUR—
IOWA

─DETOUR─
IOWA

HISTORIC DESTINATIONS

MIKE WHYE
PHOTOGRAPHY BY AUTHOR

THE
History
PRESS

Published by The History Press
Charleston, SC
www.historypress.com

All images by Mike Whye.

First published 2020

Manufactured in the United States

ISBN 9781467143455

Library of Congress Control Number: 2019954372

Notice: The information in this book is true and complete to the best of our knowledge. It is offered without guarantee on the part of the author or The History Press. The author and The History Press disclaim all liability in connection with the use of this book.

I dedicate this book to my wife, Dorie Stone, and our children, Graham, Meredith and Alex, who have accompanied me on many journeys in Iowa.

CONTENTS

11   ACKNOWLEDGEMENTS
13   INTRODUCTION

1. NORTHWEST IOWA

15   Algona
16   Lyon County
19   Manson

20   Okoboji
24   Sioux City
29   West Bend

2. WEST-CENTRAL IOWA

31   Blencoe
32   Cass County
33   Council Bluffs
39   Crescent
40   Elk Horn
42   Lewis

43   Onawa
46   Harrison County
48   Manning
49   Missouri Valley
51   Moorhead
53   Pisgah

CONTENTS

3. SOUTHWEST IOWA

55 Adair
56 Clarinda
58 Mills County
59 Greenfield
60 Mount Ayr
61 Tabor

62 Villisca
64 The Soda Fountains
of Southwest Iowa
Sidney · Corning ·
Hamburg · Shenandoah

4. NORTH-CENTRAL IOWA

69 Charles City
70 Clear Lake
74 Fort Dodge

75 Mason City
81 Rockford

5. CENTRAL IOWA

83 Boone
85 Colo
86 Des Moines Metro
Area
97 Grinnell
99 Haverhill

100 Jefferson
101 Lynnville
102 Prairie City
104 Scranton
105 Story City
106 Tama

6. SOUTH-CENTRAL IOWA

109 Allerton
110 Blakesburg
112 Eldon
116 Mahaska and Monroe
Counties

120 Ottumwa
121 Pella
126 Winterset

7. NORTHEAST IOWA

129 Burr Oak
130 Cedar Falls
131 Clayton County
131 Clermont
135 Decorah
136 Elkader
137 Festina
137 Fort Atkinson
138 Froelich

141 Independence
141 Lime Springs
142 Marquette
145 Nashua
147 New Albin
148 Quasqueton
149 Spillville
153 Waverly
155 Amish

8. EAST IOWA

157 Anamosa
158 Dubuque

162 Maquoketa
164 Quad Cities

9. EAST-CENTRAL IOWA

169 Amana
172 Cedar Rapids
174 Iowa City

176 Muscatine
178 West Branch
180 Wilton

10. SOUTHEAST IOWA

181 Burlington
182 Fort Madison
183 Keokuk
184 Louisa County

185 Montrose
185 Van Buren County
    *Bentonsport ·
    Bonaparte · Keosauqua*

191   ABOUT THE AUTHOR

ACKNOWLEDGEMENTS

I want to thank my wife, Dorie, for her help in preparing this book. She's read countless pages, put in commas, removed words, questioned my wisdom at times and helped keep my spirit going.

Thanks also to my good friend Jill Callison for her superb editing skills. She was relentless and thorough. I'm sure she, too, wondered what I was trying to write in a few places (well, okay, more than a few), and her efforts were always toward the positive, which I appreciate.

I also need to thank those who spent time talking with me and sharing their knowledge about the wonderful places in Iowa. I could not have asked for better.

INTRODUCTION

While I have written travel articles and guidebooks, those are relatively easy—learn about the fun attractions, restaurants with good food, entertaining tours, great accommodations, a bit of backstory and then write about them in a way that makes readers want to visit those places.

Writing a book about historic places, however, is a bit different because one needs to ponder, what makes a place historic? A building can be historic because of how it was designed or built or because of what someone did there, including just being born there. A patch of native prairie that's no more than three hundred acres can be historic simply because it has somehow escaped being plowed up for farmland like much of the rest of Iowa, and now it shows us what has been lost. A tour train reveals to us when passenger trains were the way to travel. We can eat at a café that fed travelers soon after the first transcontinental highway was built nearby a few years earlier. A hotel that first booked guests in 1846 will pamper us now as a bed-and-breakfast, and by driving just eight miles from there, we can visit the oldest active courthouse west of the Mississippi River. Burial mounds shaped by the loving hands of prehistoric people are, in a way, no different than a cemetery where all the headstones are identical, reminding the living that we're all alike when we come into this world and when we leave.

Then there are places we can no longer see. A twenty-seven-mile-wide crater blasted into central Iowa seventy-four million years ago by a meteorite that literally shook our world is not visible anymore—however, it was revealed partially by the soft water produced by the shattered rocks deep beneath the farmland. In another area, limestone foundations are nearly all that's left of a fort that was the only one of its kind; it was built to enforce the peace between factions of Native Americans at war with each other.

A recipe that originated in Russia centuries ago is used now to feed thousands of people a day. Cold drinks and ice cream delight the eyes and taste buds of those who visit old-time soda fountains that are still pumping frothy concoctions. One business offers up to twenty thousand types of seeds that have come from fruits, vegetables and flowers that grew in distant lands long ago and are preserved so we can use them today.

What's historic to one person may not be to another. Also, a person's mind might change upon reading something or visiting somewhere. History may be in the past, but it's always with us as we live.

I ARRANGED THIS BOOK to relate closely to "Travel Iowa," the travel guide produced by the Iowa Tourism Office. So, when readers see the places I discuss in chapter 1, "Northwest Iowa," they are in the travel guide's section about Northwest Iowa. And so it goes with the rest of my book and the travel guide, which also lists places to see, eat and stay in those areas.

"Travel Iowa" and a state map by the Iowa Department of Transportation can be ordered by contacting the Iowa Tourism Office at https://www.traveliowa.com/travelGuide or 800-345-IOWA (4692).

1

NORTHWEST IOWA

ALGONA

Henry Adams Building

Chicago architect Louis Sullivan (1856–1924) was known as the Father of the Skyscraper. He also was known for designing a series of eight buildings, mostly banks, in small towns across the Midwest. Iowa has three of the buildings—the others are in Grinnell and Cedar Rapids. To reflect the purpose of most of these buildings, Sullivan called them Jewel Boxes, and they were built between 1909 and 1919. Each appears solid, made of brick yet trimmed with colorful tile and terra-cotta ornaments. Natural light pours through large windows.

The one-story Henry Adams Building in Algona (population 5,468) was supposed to be a bank, but owner Henry C. Adams failed to obtain a charter, so it became an office building when it opened in 1913. After he departed, other businesses occupied it. Many altered it in some way, lessening its luster with each change. In 1986, the men's clothing store occupying the building declared bankruptcy and sold the nine tall stained-glass windows in a side wall to a Chicago bank. The terra-cotta planters and the stained-glass windows at the entry went for $40,000 in an auction.

Finally, Algona's nonprofit Sullivan Building Foundation purchased it in 1995 and then raised money for its restoration. Three original stained-glass windows from the east wall were donated by the Chicago bank, and reproductions of the other six were made. The foundation purchased the original windows that had been on the front wall so they could be reinstalled. Reproductions of the planters were made. Ceramic details were reproduced. A stencil on the ceiling, unseen for years, was revealed. Local craftsmen re-created the furnishings designed by Sullivan. After eighteen years and $800,000, the restoration opened in 2013, one hundred years after it began business.

The Algona Chamber of Commerce now occupies the building.

POW Nativity

During World War II, Algona had one of two prisoner-of-war camps in Iowa. Each held about three thousand prisoners, mostly Germans. Rather than let the prisoners languish in the camps, authorities put many to work to relieve the manpower shortage the war had caused in the United States. In 1943, Iowa had about seventy thousand fewer people working in agriculture than before the war, and the POWs eased the strain.

The Algona camp opened in April 1944, and a few months later, German POW Edward Kaib arrived. Using baked soil, he created a small nativity in the camp that impressed the commander so much that he asked Kaib to build a larger one. Kaib and five other Germans worked for months on the new one, fashioning the scene and sixty-five figures out of wood, wire, plaster and concrete. In December 1945, the Germans presented the half-life-size nativity to the people of Algona. (Even though the war in Europe had ended in May 1945, many POWs remained in the camps until months later.) When the POWs left, the nativity was transferred to a building on the Kossuth County Fairgrounds, where it remains.

The nativity is open only from the first Sunday in December through New Year's Day. The First United Methodist Church in Algona administers the site.

LYON COUNTY

Gitchie Manitou State Preserve

The oldest rocks in Iowa are easily seen in Gitchie Manitou State Preserve, tucked into the state's northwest corner. Although commonly found in parts of neighboring South Dakota and Minnesota, the pink, red and purple

Sioux quartzite rocks are visible nowhere else in Iowa. They are estimated to be about 1.6 billion years old, give or take a millennium. In many places, the rocks have fractured naturally in such a way that they look like they were carved into steps.

The north entrance is near a parking area that's big enough for just a few vehicles near a private residence. The parking lot is at the juncture of 100th Street (County Highway K10) and South Dakota Highway 115. A footpath leads west from the parking lot into the preserve, which is a mix of the rocks (mostly in the northern end), prairie grasses and some areas shaded by trees. Prickly pear cactus, which can penetrate soft shoes, is on the rocks and in the prairie grass.

The remains of an old picnic shelter made of the rock are here, but the most fun is just exploring the rocks, checking out the lichen and the tiny plants that grow among the smooth—but still hard—surfaces of the rocks.

The preserve's other entrance is three-quarters of a mile south of the north entrance and can be accessed by following County Highway K10 to the south.

Blood Run National Historic Site

Blood Run National Historic Landmark is a short drive from the south entrance of Gitchie Manitou. Visitors should follow the main road south to where it turns east and then south on Iowa K10 (Apple Avenue). A mile later, visitors should turn west on 120th Street, a gravel road. That soon turns to the south and ends at a closed auto gate. From there, people explore the 178-acre site on foot.

Although evidence has been found to suggest the site—where Blood Run Creek meets the Big Sioux River—had been used as far back as 6500 BC, perhaps its most important time was between AD 1500 and 1714, when five thousand or more members of the Oneota culture lived here. Native Americans related to the Oneota culture are the Omaha, Winnebago, Oto, Missouria, Ioway, Osage, Kansa and Ponca. Dakota, Arikara and Cheyenne may have visited here. Archaeologists believe the Oneota village covered about 1,200 acres, encompassing this site and some land across the Big Sioux River in South Dakota.

The site was named by Native Americans who believed the waters of Blood Run Creek ran red with blood at times. Actually, rusting particles of iron in the surrounding soils tinted the waters.

No explanation is known for the pits carved into this boulder at Blood Run National Historic Site, where a village of up to five thousand members of the Oneota culture lasted until about 1714.

Residents of Blood Run used tools of bone and stone to prepare food from the corn, squash, beans and other vegetables and fruit raised here. Pottery made here was used for storage. Game hunted in the region was brought to the village to be made into food, clothing and articles for trade.

Items from across the plains have been recovered at Blood Run, indicating that it was a trade center. Catlinite, also called pipestone, was quarried about forty miles away and used here in trading, as archaeologists have found many examples of it, ranging from small pipes to engraved plaques.

Only a few items that indicate work done by metal tools—which were used only by European Americans—have been found here. It's believed they arrived here as a series of trades that began far to the east with the Europeans.

Pits were dug to hold food, pottery and hides for later use. When these cache pits were emptied, garbage was thrown in them and they were covered with dirt.

Some houses were round and others rectangular, oval or square. The residents also created burial mounds. In 1889, a mapmaker counted 276 mounds in Blood Run. Because of European American agricultural practices and quarry companies attracted by the gravel-laden soils, only 76 mounds remain, and they are difficult to see. Supposedly, several low linear mounds were fashioned like a serpent in one area of Blood Run. It, too, has disappeared. One item easily seen is a boulder about the size of a stuffed chair. At the site's southern border, it is covered with small pits—about the width of golf balls—that no one can explain except to say they were made by humans.

At the auto gate, visitors can hike a two-mile trail that loops back to the gate—an extension trail leads to the pitted boulder. Lyon County Conservation Board administers the site.

Collecting and digging are forbidden here. Plans exist to further develop this Iowa site into part of a state park shared by Iowa and South Dakota, where that state's portion is already developed as Good Earth State Park.

MANSON

Manson Impact Crater

About four miles north of Manson (population 1,589) is the center of the nation's largest meteor impact crater. It's also the world's fifteenth largest, measuring about twenty-seven miles wide and five and a half miles deep. It was created by a meteor estimated to be up to two miles wide that was traveling about forty-five thousand miles an hour when it hit here seventy-four million years ago. The debris ejected into the atmosphere killed all life for hundreds of miles around. Evidence of the impact has been found in Nebraska and South Dakota. Reminiscent of photos of moon craters, the ground rebounded from the collision and forced up a section of granite that had been two to four miles deep to create a mound in the center of the crater.

Yet those who drive to southeast Pocahontas County expecting to see a deep crater won't see anything like that. No one in a plane will see anything either. That's because since the meteorite hit, the forces of nature have filled the crater with sediment to the point that the crater floor is now sixty to three hundred feet below the land's surface. The top of the crater's central mound is about ninety feet below the surface.

So, with nothing to see, how did anyone know a crater was here? People drilling for water in the early twentieth century encountered deformed rock unlike that found in the surrounding terrain. Some wondered if some volcanic activity had taken place here. Beginning in 1959, scientists began studying the soils in this area and found shocked quartz grains, which are made by nuclear weapons, lightning strikes and meteorites. That ruled out the possibility of volcanic activity.

About the only clue that a huge meteor hit here is the town sign on the edge of Manson, which reads, "Making an Impact." An interesting fact about the meteorite is that because it destroyed the region's limestone—which helps to create hard water throughout the rest of Iowa—the water in this area has been soft all these millions of years, and Manson is known as the soft water capital of the world.

OKOBOJI

Abbie Gardner Sharp Cabin

The word Okoboji (Oak-oh-boh-jee) means basically one thing in today's Iowa—an area of spring-fed lakes in northwest Iowa that is the state's premier summertime playground. The three principal bodies of water are Spirit Lake, the state's largest natural lake; West Lake Okoboji, the second-largest natural lake; and East Lake Okoboji, the fifth-largest natural lake in Iowa.

Even though Okoboji is singular, it represents the region; in the mid-nineteenth century it was collectively called Spirit Lake.

In a tree-shaded park in the small community of Arnolds Park, the log cabin at the Abbie Gardner Sharp State Historic Site is a reminder of one of the sadder chapters in Iowa history—the Spirit Lake Massacre. For years, the massacre was described as a simple matter—several Dakota killed most of the settlers here in the spring of 1857. However, the story is more complex.

When twelve-year-old Abbie Gardner arrived with her family on the shores of West Lake Okoboji in July 1856, they were the first of fifty or so settlers in the region. Their seventeen-by-twenty-three-foot one-room log cabin was much like the other structures being built there.

On the morning of March 8, 1857, when Abbie was about to eat breakfast with her family and some friends, an Indian man entered the cabin. Because of the harsh winter that was finally breaking for a while, the Gardners figured he was hungry like them and prepared a place for him at the table.

The Abbie Gardner Sharp cabin, now a state historic site on the south shore of West Lake Okoboji, is where Lakota-settler relations turned deadly in 1857.

Then thirteen other Indian men arrived. They, too, accepted food offered to them. Then they grew belligerent, demanding ammunition and gunpowder. Indian women and children showed up too. The settlers had no way of knowing that they were members of a small band of Dakota called Wahpekute, for they had never met prior to that day.

For various reasons, the Wahpekute rarely mixed with their Dakota relatives. Rarely taking supplies distributed by the U.S. government, they subsisted off the land while traveling over what became southern Minnesota, northwest Iowa and eastern South Dakota. As time went on, more disagreements divided the Wahpekute again, with the smaller faction following their leader, Sintominaduta, who was aided by a warrior named Inkpaduta. Settlers who met Inkpaduta described him as six feet tall, powerfully built and having a menacing look, perhaps because smallpox had scarred his face.

Sintominaduta's band had mixed relations with the whites coming into the region more and more beginning in the 1840s. Some settlers accused the Wahpekute of stealing from them. On the other hand, in 1848, five of Sintominaduta's ponies were found in the possession of Henry Lott, a known horse thief. Fearing what the Wahpekute might do to him, Lott fled the area for several years, although he left behind his wife and children.

In his absence, his wife and a son died. Lott spun tales that they had been killed by the Wahpekute, but many whites knew his tales were lies.

The Wahpekute got along with many whites, including the sutler at Fort Dodge, an army post built in 1850, and settlers and fur trapper Curtis Lamb, who arrived in Smithland (southeast of present-day Sioux City) in 1851. From then until 1853, the Wahpekute wintered near the Lamb farm. They prepared a garden for the Lamb family and supplied them with firewood, furs and eggs from geese and ducks that Lamb then traded for cash at Kanesville (present-day Council Bluffs). Sintominaduta sent two of his children to a white school in Minnesota, where they were regarded as good students.

Lott returned to the area near Fort Dodge in 1854 and, with some followers, killed Sintominaduta and five of his family. Inkpaduta demanded justice, and although a white grand jury indicted Lott for the killings, he fled once more, this time forever. Angered by what he regarded as the whites' refusal to punish Lott, Inkpaduta was further upset when he saw Sintominaduta's skull had been nailed to a post by a white man. In revenge, he and his followers plundered the cabins of some settlers in the area but later returned some of the stolen items.

During these years, life for the Dakota in the area was becoming harder. They had been watching white settlers enter their territory, pushing them and other Native Americans farther west. Also, the influx of whites diminished the game that the Native Americans had hunted there forever. By 1855, settlers around Cherokee, about forty-five miles southwest of Spirit Lake, reported seeing no buffalo anymore. Elk were becoming scarce.

Inkpaduta's band returned to Smithland in December 1856, just as a winter storm was arriving. Once there, they learned Curtis Lamb had moved on, and even though the new owner of Lamb's farm did not like the Wahpekute, some of the whites in the area remained friendly.

However, when Wahpekute women were seen scavenging leftover corn in the fields one day, food that some whites also coveted that winter, those whites beat the women. Not long afterward, a warrior who was hunting elk killed a settler's dog that attacked him. Angered by the killing, twenty whites set upon the Wahpekute camp, forcing those in the camp to leave. Despite Inkpaduta's pleas that the Wahpekute needed their guns to hunt game, the whites took the weapons from the Indians.

Away from Smithland, the Wahpekute again split their numbers. About eighty warriors, women and children went with Inkpaduta to follow the Little Sioux River to the northeast and its headwaters—Spirit Lake.

Along the way, they stole guns, ammunition, gunpowder and food at some settlements. They killed settlers' pigs and cattle, not for food but out of anger. At the small settlement of Peterson, where they had previously had good relations, they plundered the place and raped three women. Although they left some whites unharmed, the Wahpekute beat many who they met. At another settlement, they kidnapped two women before releasing them the next day. In one attack, a settler killed a warrior, yet by the time the Wahpekute reached Spirit Lake on the evening of March 7, they had killed no one.

The next morning, they approached the Gardners' cabin, and in a short time, the killing began. Before the Wahpekute left five days later, thirty-two settlers were dead, and they took Abbie Gardner and three women as captives. Word of the massacre spread from Dakota who were friendly with whites and a white man who stumbled upon the carnage. Still, some who were warned did not believe the stories. These included three brothers who operated a trading post near Springfield (now Jackson, Minnesota), eighteen miles from Spirit Lake. On March 20, two of Inkpaduta's band used eighty dollars in gold coins, taken from a Spirit Lake cabin, to buy supplies, including guns and ammunition at the trading post.

Six days later, the Wahpekute struck Springfield, where forty-seven settlers lived. A group who believed the warnings had fortified two log cabins, while others stayed in their own cabins. Seven settlers died, including the three brothers at the trading post. That night, several settlers escaped, fleeing in horse-drawn sleds across the wintry landscape to reach Fort Dodge two days later.

Gardner and the three women held captive with her were forced to carry burdensome packs and trudge through the snow while the Wahpekute women wore snowshoes and the warriors rode horses. When Inkpaduta's band left the region, nearly forty settlers at Spirit Lake and Springfield were dead and more wounded.

As the band wandered, mostly going west into Dakota Territory, the captors killed two of the women. The third was released in early May. After eighty-four days of captivity, Gardner was traded for two horses, twelve blankets, two kegs of gunpowder, thirty-two yards of cloth, ribbons and twenty pounds of tobacco.

When she returned to the family cabin in July 1857, a pastor had acquired it and refused to give it back to her. Because females had no rights at that time, she could not file a claim against the minister. However, in 1891, she bought it and turned it into a tourist attraction where she sold copies of her book, *History of the Spirit Lake Massacre and Captivity of Miss Abbie Gardner.*

When she died in 1921, she was buried with her relatives near the cabin. The cabin is now an Iowa State Historic Site.

Inkpaduta was never caught. For years, his name was dreaded by whites, as he was said to be everywhere on the plains. Some people said he was at the Battle of the Little Bighorn, although he was too infirm to participate in it. He died in 1881 in Manitoba, Canada.

Although the area where most of the killings occurred was called Spirit Lake, not all that many years later, people began calling the region Okoboji, and the name stuck.

Amusement Park at Arnolds Park

In 1930, construction began on a wood-frame roller coaster that, with improvements, still produces excitement and shrieks of joy many times a day each summer in the Amusement Park. Now called the Legend, it's the seventh-oldest roller coaster in the United States and thirteenth oldest in the world. The amusement park has at least twenty other rides, ranging from those that will have the kids giggling to eye-opening thrillers such as the Log Flume and the Wild Mouse, one of the oldest in existence.

SIOUX CITY

Loess Hills

A narrow band of hills that range from 3 to 15 miles wide, the Loess Hills run down Iowa's west side from an area about 20 miles north of Sioux City to near St. Joseph, Missouri, 220 miles away. While loess soils are found in many places around the world, nowhere else but China's Huangtu Plateau are loess deposits as deep as those in western Iowa.

As the last ice age was ending, between ten and fourteen thousand years ago, the glaciers that had covered much of the earth began to retreat bit by bit as the climate warmed. While receding, they revealed the silt that they had created by grinding everything they had moved across into powder. In this area, runoff from the melting glaciers carried away this finely ground soil—called loess (it rhymes with bus)—which, when dry, was lifted aloft by winds to places near and far. While some loess measuring a few inches deep is found hundreds of miles away, the largest concentrations of the silt fell from the sky near the rivers of runoff in what would become the Missouri River valley, and slowly dunes began to appear. Over thousands of years, those dunes close to the river grew to be hundreds of feet higher than the floodplain.

As the hills grew, grasses took hold, stabilizing the hills and creating a prairie ecosystem that lasted for thousands of years. The few trees that existed grew around ponds, lakes and waterways and in well-watered folds in the hilly landscape. Wildfires, which rejuvenated the plant life on the prairie-topped hills, also kept the trees from encroaching on the grasslands. However, the onset of European American civilization created firebreaks in the form of farm fields, roads and communities. With fewer wildfires to cleanse the area, the hills have been nearly overtaken by trees in the last century.

The Dorothy Pecaut Nature Center on the west side of Sioux City has displays relating to the wildlife and flora in the hills along with a walk-through replica of a hill's interior. Indoor exhibits include regional reptiles and fish in an aquarium while outside are colorful butterfly and wildflower gardens. Because the free nature center is enveloped by the three-thousand-acre Stone State Park, which is situated on several of the loess hills with many lookouts across Iowa, South Dakota and Nebraska, the park's eight miles of trails are easily accessible.

Sergeant Floyd Monument

The Sergeant Floyd Monument, a one-hundred-foot-tall obelisk that stands atop a bluff south of Sioux City, marks the final resting place of Sergeant Charles M. Floyd. In 1803, he joined the expedition led by Captains Meriwether Lewis and William Clark to explore the Louisiana Purchase, which had just become part of the United States. The expedition, formally called the Corps of Discovery, left St. Louis on May 14, 1804, and three months later Floyd died of apparent appendicitis near here. He was the only member of the expedition to die during the twenty-eight-month-long exploration. The thirty-two-year-old sergeant was buried with military honors atop this bluff, which overlooks the Missouri River.

Sergeant Floyd Museum and Welcome Center

Often, welcome centers are buildings, but Sioux City uses a historical boat, the *Sergeant Floyd*, which is in Chris Larsen Park along the Missouri River between Exits 47 and 49 on I-29.

Built in 1932 along the lines of a river tug, the *Sergeant Floyd* was used by the U.S. Army Corps of Engineers as a survey and inspection boat for projects on the Missouri River. In 1983, the 138-foot-long boat was permanently landlocked in the park to become a museum and visitor center. The *Sergeant Floyd* was named after Charles M. Floyd, a member of the Lewis and Clark expedition.

On the boat, visitors climb steep, narrow steps to the glass-enclosed pilot house, which overlooks the river and a marina. When the *Sergeant Floyd* was in service, it carried a crew of thirty-two quartered in cabins on the second and third decks. Two six-hundred-horsepower diesel engines can be seen through an opening in the main deck where they rest on the lowest deck below.

Displays in the boat are split between the history of boats that have traveled the Missouri—from dugout canoes to palatial passenger ships to

Formerly a survey boat used by the U.S. Army Corps of Engineers on the Missouri River, the *Sergeant Floyd* is now a Sioux City riverboat museum and welcome center.

today's barges—and the Lewis and Clark expedition that passed here in 1804 and 1806. Included in the displays are maps, historic photos and a life-sized figure of Charles Floyd created by a forensic artist.

In the rear of the main deck, the tourist information center is loaded with information about local and regional attractions, lodgings and places to eat.

Nearby, the Lewis and Clark Interpretive Center has many good displays about the expedition that went to the West Coast and back between 1804 and 1806.

Sioux City Railroad Museum

Railroads have played a major role in Sioux City since a train first came here in 1868. In the 1920s, Sioux City was the tenth-largest railroad hub in the nation, with six major railroads operating here.

One of those, the Chicago, Milwaukee, St. Paul and Pacific Railroad, also called the Milwaukee Road, built a major repair facility in the city's Riverside district in 1918. Part of the facility was a thirty-stall building used to maintain steam locomotives. The engine repair shop was arranged in a half circle around a turntable that allowed each engine to arrive from a railroad track and then be directed into a stall. At one time, six hundred men served thirty-five locomotives every day.

A volunteer at the Sioux City Railroad Museum stands near a steam locomotive built in 1909 for the Great Northern Railroad.

In 1954, many of the buildings on the property and more than half of the roundhouse were torn down. Today, six stalls remain in the roundhouse, and the turntable is still operational. The roundhouse is one of just seven such structures still standing in the nation. One stall in the roundhouse shelters the museum's premier attraction, a steam locomotive built in 1909 for the Great Northern Railroad, which used it for forty-five years before retiring it. Although not operational, the beautiful green, silver and black locomotive is sometimes moved onto the turntable by a small switch engine. The museum also has boxcars, a baggage car, cabooses and a 1947 dining car that has been restored and is used for hosting dinners and afternoon teas.

About a dozen other historic buildings, such as a machine shop and a shop to repair railroad cars, are on the museum's thirty-acre property. The museum also has elaborate HO-, O- and N-gauge model railroad layouts.

Woodbury County Courthouse

Courthouses across the United States come in a variety of styles but quite often are Greek Revival, Italianate, Beaux-Arts and Romanesque. Sioux City's Woodbury County Courthouse is in a class of its own called Prairie School. The largest Prairie School–style building anywhere, it was built in 1918 and designed by local architect William K. Steele, who collaborated with Minneapolis architects George Grant Elmslie and William Gray Purcell, all proponents of the Prairie School style. An eight-story tower rises out of a square four-story base that has colorful tile murals, a goldfish pond and a stained-glass rotunda. Prairie School architecture came about in the early twentieth century and made use of the horizontal lines of the prairie plus open floor plans and local materials.

Built in 1918, the Woodbury County Courthouse in Sioux City is the world's largest example of Prairie School architecture.

WEST BEND

Grotto of the Redemption

The town of West Bend has what is believed to be the world's largest grotto. The Grotto of the Redemption had its beginnings when a German immigrant came down with pneumonia while studying for the priesthood in Milwaukee, Wisconsin. Paul Matthias Dobberstein promised the Virgin Mary that he would build a grotto in her honor when he recovered. In 1898, he became a pastor in West Bend and began to build the grotto in 1912.

Dobberstein collected rocks from across the world for the grotto. Railroad cars of various minerals arrived in West Bend, where Dobberstein and an assistant unloaded the rocks, sorted them and precisely placed each one according to the priest's plans to create nine grottos to depict the life of Jesus. When Dobberstein died in 1954, another priest continued the construction until declaring it finished in 2004. Among the materials are jasper, quartz, rubies, agates, petrified wood, geodes and malachite. The grotto claims to have the largest collection of precious and semiprecious stones in the world and is worth more than $4 million.

2

WEST-CENTRAL IOWA

BLENCOE

Loess Hills Overlook

One of the better overlooks of the Loess Hills is about eight miles east of Blencoe, at Exit 105 on I-29. A footpath leads from a wooden viewing platform to the south across hills topped with native prairie.

To visit the overlook, drive Highway E60 from Blencoe to Highway L14 about seven and a half miles away. Then turn left (north) to go three miles to 286th Street. There, turn right (east) and enter the hills. In less than a half mile, bear right at the Y intersection onto Oak Avenue, which reaches the overlook less than three miles later.

Hikers take to a trail that leads across the prairie-topped Loess Hills east of Blencoe. The hills were formed by windblown soils after the last ice age ended between ten and fourteen thousand years ago.

CASS COUNTY

Tree in the Middle of the Road

Sometimes something becomes famous for just being where it is, and that's the case for a tree that stands on the border between Cass and Audubon Counties. It's also in the middle of an intersection—hence its well-earned name: Tree in the Middle of the Road. Iowans call them as they see them.

The story about this tree is that a surveyor cut a young cottonwood to use as a walking stick when on the job in 1850. At some point, he needed to mark a survey point and, having nothing else at hand, stuck the young cottonwood in the dirt. Prairie was tilled into agricultural land and roads were created, but everyone left the cottonwood alone. It may be one hundred feet tall now.

An easy way to the tree is to leave I-80 at Exit 64 and go south less than half a mile to County Road G16, also called Boston Road. Turn left (east) and drive about two miles to 710th Street. Turn left and drive north for one mile to the tree. There's no way anyone can miss the tree, although everyone hopes all drivers do miss it.

Accidentally planted by a surveyor in 1850, a cottonwood stands tall in an intersection of country roads on the border of Cass and Audubon Counties.

COUNCIL BLUFFS

What's in a Name?

Council Bluffs has a different name than when it was founded. Native Americans had lived here for countless years, with the last group, about two thousand Potawatami arriving in the 1830s, having been forced out of their Chicago-area homeland when they ended up on the losing side of the War of 1812. Their leader, Sauganash, was the son of a Potawatami mother and a Scottish-Irish immigrant. He was also known as Billy Caldwell, and the region was called Camp Caldwell or Billy Caldwell's Camp for a few years.

In 1844, ten Iowa families traveled through here by wagon on their way to Oregon, beginning what would soon be a major trail west. At about the same time, members of the Church of Jesus Christ of Latter-day Saints, also known as Mormons, began arriving in the area, as they were fleeing troubles in Illinois and heading west to Utah.

Because the land was then an Indian reservation, a non-Mormon, Thomas Kane, arranged permission from the federal government for the Mormons to temporarily live here. To honor Kane, the Mormons renamed the area Kanesville.

In 1847, the Mormons built a log structure in Kanesville as their first tabernacle, and it was here that about one thousand members chose Brigham Young as president of their church. Unfortunately, the building was built over a spring and was used for only two years before it needed to be torn down.

The Kanesville Tabernacle, a 1996 replica of the earlier one, is just east of downtown CB (as locals sometimes call their town). Run by the Church of Jesus Christ of Latter-day Saints, it's close to the original site.

By 1852, most of the Mormons had left, and the citizens of Kanesville decided to rename their town. The name Council Bluffs had been applied to this region of the Missouri River valley in honor of the council that explorers Lewis and Clark had held with area Indians in 1804. Although the council was held sixteen miles upriver and on the Nebraska side of the river, Council Bluffs became the community's new name.

Bregant House

The Bregant House at 517 Fourth Street is unique in that it was designed for its original owners, Jean and Inez Bregant. Jean was forty-five inches tall, Inez, forty-two. They met on the vaudeville circuit and chose to make Council Bluffs their home when they married in 1905. They purchased the lot next to Inez's parents' home and completed construction of their one-story, scaled-down house in 1912. Built as a Craftsman-style bungalow, its doorknobs, light switches, kitchen appliances, fireplace mantel and cabinets were set lower than normal. The bathtub was shorter too. However, most of the furniture is sized to accommodate the Bregants' guests. For some years, the couple traveled a twenty-state region promoting Woodward Candy Company, which was based in Council Bluffs. Jean died in 1955 and Inez in 1969. The Historical Society of Pottawattamie County owns the house.

Golden Spike Monument

Standing fifty-six feet tall and shaped like a railroad spike, the Golden Spike Monument is painted gold to honor the one that was used to complete the Transcontinental Railroad in Utah. The monument stands at Milepost 0, the eastern terminus of the famous railroad.

Although the Transcontinental Railroad was declared complete during the ceremony at Promontory Summit, Utah, on May 10, 1869, it was transcontinental in name only because no bridge then crossed the Missouri River to connect the railroad tracks in Council Bluffs with those in Omaha. Until 1873, when a bridge finally spanned the Missouri there, passengers coming from either direction had to leave their trains, ride a ferry across the river and then catch trains on the other side of the river to continue to their destinations.

Still, the opening of the bridge did not make this route the first railroad to physically cross the United States. That distinction belongs to the Kansas Pacific Railroad, which crossed the plains to connect with other railroads on June 30, 1869. From that time on, anyone could travel from the Atlantic to the Pacific by railroad.

Historic General Dodge House and the Black Angel

On a hillside overlooking the valley of the Missouri River, the Historic General Dodge House was built for Grenville Dodge in 1869 at the cost of $35,000. A Massachusetts native, Dodge moved to Council Bluffs at the age of twenty in 1851. Initially, he worked as a surveyor for various railroads, including the Union Pacific Railroad. Then he served with distinction in the Union army during the Civil War and was known for his work organizing railroads and intelligence operations. In 1866, he became the chief engineer for the Union Pacific and helped to establish the route of the first transcontinental railroad. He engaged in banking and politics but remained heavily involved with railroads, serving as president of several railroad companies.

The three-story home with the mansard roof boasted various innovations for its time, including central heating, marble sinks with hot and cold running water and a flush toilet, perhaps the first in the city. When the last of the general's children died in 1950, the executor of her estate offered the house to the city, but her offer was refused. What original furnishings were not taken by the Dodge descendants were auctioned off, as was the home, which was changed into an apartment house.

In 1963, the city bought the house and slowly began refurnishing it with items representative of the house's most prominent time. The main floor has twin parlors, a private study, a dining room, a kitchen and a sun porch. Bedrooms occupy the second floor, and there is a ballroom on the third floor.

Tours of the Dodge House begin in the August Beresheim House, immediately to the south, which was built in 1899 for one of Dodge's banking partners.

Although many Council Bluffs residents consider Dodge to be the city's most illustrious resident, it's likely few can say where he's buried. The same almost goes for his wife, Ruth Anne Dodge, who died eight months after he did. However, ask for the location of the Black Angel—which is the nickname for the memorial where she is buried—and most will know. Shortly before Ruth Anne passed away of cancer, she shared some dreams with her daughters. In one, a winged angel stood on the prow of a boat while holding a bowl of water for Ruth Anne to drink. After she died in 1916, the daughters commissioned famed sculptor Daniel Chester French, who would sculpt the seated Abraham Lincoln memorial statue in Washington, D.C., to create the angel of their mother's dreams. Officially called the Ruth Anne Dodge Memorial, it's the only statue created by French in Iowa.

Above: The Historic General Dodge House in Council Bluffs was built in 1869 at a cost of $35,000 and features twin parlors and the city's first flush toilet.

Right: Nicknamed the Black Angel, a bronze statue crafted by famed sculptor Daniel Chester French, marks the grave of Ruth Anne Dodge, who spoke of dreaming about the angel shortly before she died.

Made of cast bronze, the statue darkens between periodic refurbishments, which has spawned legends and led to some calling it the Black Angel. The most prevalent story is that anyone who kisses her will die within a day. Although she stands alongside a cemetery, it's doubtful that anyone at rest there kissed the statue to gain entry. Still, one might not want to suffer pained lips by attempting to kiss her on hot summer days or freezing winter nights.

Lincoln Monument

At the west end of Lafayette Avenue is the Lincoln Monument, a granite spire that rises above a brick-and-concrete plaza sitting atop a bluff overlooking the Missouri River floodplain. In August 1859, Abraham Lincoln came to Council Bluffs on a steamboat from St. Joseph, Missouri, on private business for a friend. At this time, Lincoln had been a U.S. representative from Illinois and then returned to his law practice in Springfield, Illinois, where he became a rising star in the Republican Party. His antislavery "House Divided" speech had garnered lots of attention, as did his seven debates with Stephen A. Douglas for the Illinois U.S. Senate seat.

On his first evening in town, after receiving many requests to speak, Lincoln addressed an overflow crowd in a meeting hall. The next morning, he rode in an open carriage with friends to the west end of Lafayette Avenue, where an overlook gave a view for miles to the west, north and south. The men with Lincoln advocated that this was the perfect place to begin constructing the transcontinental railroad to the west. Grenville Dodge was with Lincoln that day. Although only twenty-eight then, Dodge had been surveying the lands to the west and told Lincoln that this was the best place for the eastern terminus of the Transcontinental Railroad.

On July 1, 1862, Lincoln, then president of the United States, signed the Pacific Railroad Act, which authorized the construction of the Transcontinental Railroad and designated Council Bluffs as its eastern terminus.

Runza

What is a runza, readers living beyond western Iowa and Nebraska may wonder. People who know may wonder why it's in a book about historical places? To answer both questions—it's akin to a stuffed bread with a centuries-old history.

The runza (pronounced run-zah) has its origins in the eighteenth century when Russian empress Catherine the Great, born in Germany, offered Germans to come to Russia to enjoy a life with religious freedom, no military conscript, no taxes for thirty years and self-governance in their communities. More than 100,000 Germans took her up on the offer and moved to Russia between 1763 and 1871. During that time, they became successful farmers and cattle breeders, and their numbers grew.

After Catherine died in 1796, the succeeding czars were not as friendly toward their new countrymen. In 1871, Czar Alexander II came down harshly on the German immigrants, and they decided to leave for North and South America. More than 300,000 came to the United States. The largest group, 19,000, settled in Nebraska. Along with their strong work ethics, they brought their favorite foods, including a pocket bread stuffed with beef, cabbage, onion and spices. Sometimes sauerkraut was substituted for cabbage in these breads, which were known by various names, including bierock, krautburger, kraut pirok and runza.

Siblings Sarah "Sally" Everett and Alex Brening used their family's runza recipe and opened the first Runza Drive-In in Lincoln, Nebraska, in 1949. More than eighty Runza Restaurants are now serving meals. The majority are in Nebraska. Two are in Iowa. One is on West Broadway in Council Bluffs, and the other is on South Sixteenth Street in Clarinda.

Squirrel Cage Jail

The outside of the former Pottawattamie County Jail looks like many other brick buildings built in the 1880s. Inside the three-story building is an equally tall, drum-like set of thirty barred jail cells—with ten cells on each level—that gave the place its nickname, the Squirrel Cage Jail.

The jail was one of eighteen of similar design built in the United States. Now, just three survive, with the other two in Missouri and Indiana. These jails featured a cylindrical set of cells with each resembling a slice of pie. Around that three-story drum of cells was a stationary set of bars that had only one gated

Originally, the three-story set of drum-like cells rotated so only one cell faced an opening on each floor of Council Bluffs' Squirrel Cage Jail.

opening on each floor. When the jailer wanted to move an inmate in or out of a cell, the drum was rotated until that cell faced one of the gated openings, and then door there was unlatched.

The system may have seemed efficient in that only a few jailers were needed to operate the jail, which was considered escape-proof. However, in 1969, the jail was closed because prisoners could not be evacuated safely in case of fire.

Union Pacific Railroad Museum

The Union Pacific Railroad Museum is in the former city library, which the Carnegie Foundation donated to the city in 1905. It was the largest Carnegie library in Iowa. While the Beaux-Arts exterior is much as it was, most of the original interior is hidden behind renovations.

The museum's prize possession is a silver set—a water pitcher, two goblets and a samovar to heat water—that was destined to be in a special train car used by President Abraham Lincoln. However, he was assassinated before using the car, and it became the funeral car that carried his body through several states before he was buried in Springfield, Illinois. The museum's other displays relate to traveling across the United States before railroads tied it together and the history of constructing the first Transcontinental Railroad which started west from Council Bluffs. More exhibits are about when passenger trains were *the* way to travel. Different place settings of fine china used in the dining cars are here with menus. One touts "Charcoal Broiled Filet Mignon Bordelaise $4.60."

The museum has one of the four ceremonial spikes used to mark the completion of the Transcontinental Railroad when the UP's tracks met those of the Central Pacific Railroad at Promontory Summit, Utah.

CRESCENT

Hitchcock Nature Center

Located about five miles north of Crescent, the 1,268-acre Hitchcock Nature Center contains ten miles of trails that wander through woods and prairie. Badger Ridge Trail, in particular, traverses parts of the hills that look like

Ten miles of trails lead across prairie and through woods in the 1,268-acre Hitchcock Nature Center near the town of Crescent.

they did when all of the hills were covered with prairie two centuries ago. A lodge and educational programs explain the history of the Loess Hills in this area. Adjacent to the lodge, a fifty-foot-high tower serves as a good viewpoint, and it's where birdwatchers participate in the nationwide Hawk Watch program each fall.

ELK HORN

Danish Windmill

Many residents of Elk Horn and Kimballton are descendants of Danish immigrants who arrived in Iowa mostly between 1880 and 1920 and created the largest rural Danish settlement in the United States. To honor their heritage during the country's bicentennial, a group of residents arranged to disassemble, ship and reassemble a windmill that had been built in Denmark in 1846.

Stone-ground flour and rye, made in the windmill, are available in the gift shop, and tours can be arranged.

Built in 1846 in Denmark, this windmill was brought to Elk Horn to celebrate the heritage of those in the largest rural Danish settlement in the U.S.

The Museum of Danish America is about a mile from the windmill in a building that looks like it belongs on a farm in Denmark. More than thirty-five thousand artifacts relating to Denmark are here along with stories of the immigrants and Danish American life.

In town, the museum also maintains Bedstemor's House, which is furnished to resemble the home of a Danish grandmother of a century ago.

Elk Horn celebrates two Danish events each year. Tivoli Fest is held the Saturday and Sunday of the Memorial Day weekend, and Julefest is held the Friday, Saturday and Sunday of Thanksgiving weekend.

Two miles north of Elk Horn is Kimballton, a smaller community. A replica of *The Little Mermaid* statue in Copenhagen's harbor and based on the tale by Hans Christian Andersen is in a fountain in town's small business district.

LEWIS

Hitchcock House

In 1856, when the Reverend George Hitchcock built this two-story sandstone home on a hill overlooking the East Nishnabotna River, Iowa was free state that did not permit slavery. However, that did not mean slaves who reached Iowa were safe, because federal laws permitted slave hunters to go anywhere in the United States to find runaway slaves and return them to their owners. The farther slaves could travel away from the slave states the better. Since Hitchcock's house, just outside of Lewis, was less than fifty miles from the Missouri border, it was never going to be a destination.

Instead, it was a stop on what was called the Underground Railroad. Neither a real railroad nor underground, it was a web of secret routes and safe places scattered

The home built near Lewis by the Reverend George Hitchcock in 1856 was a safe rest for slaves fleeing to freedom on secret routes called the Underground Railroad.

through the free states. Slaves used the Underground Railroad to flee bounty hunters. Some settled in Canada. It's estimated up to 100,000 slaves gained their freedom by 1850. No one knows how many passed through Iowa on their way east and north.

Helping runaway slaves was dangerous. Anyone found sheltering them could be imprisoned for up to six months and fined $1,000 (about $2,900 now).

Hitchcock's house might have looked like it had a full basement to any slave hunters who looked in it. However, a hinged cupboard hid a secret area used by slaves.

The Nishnabotna Ferry House

In 1850, a ferry was operating at this site at the East Nishnabotna River, but it went out of business when a bridge was built across the river a short time later for people traveling between Council Bluffs and Des Moines. However, the bridge collapsed in 1856, and the ferry was once more in business. In 1857, Samuel Tefft and his family moved into the small white house that had been built on the east bank of the river, and he took over the toll ferry.

It's not known how much Tefft charged for people, horses and wagons, but in one five-month period, he collected ninety-eight dollars in tolls. Tefft possibly earned a lot of money because nearly three thousand members of the Church of Jesus Christ of Latter-day Saints pushing handcarts passed through here from 1856 to 1860.

In 1859, a new bridge was built over the river, and again the ferry ceased operating. That same year, abolitionist John Brown and other whites escorted a group of eighteen slaves across the river here.

ONAWA

Lewis and Clark State Park

The entrance to Lewis and Clark State Park is about four miles west of Onawa on State Highway 175. The expedition led by Lewis and Clark camped here on the night of August 9, 1804. While here, Lewis wrote in his journal about a sight the men had seen on the Missouri River the previous day. (The following contains his spellings and phraseology.)

I saw a great number of feathers floating down the river—those feathers had a very extraordinary appearance as they appeared in such quantities as to cover pretty generally sixty or seventy yards of the breadth of the river. for three miles after I saw those feathers continuing to run in that manner, we did not percieve from whence they came, at length we were surprised by the appearance of a flock of Pillican at rest on a large sand bar attatched to a small Island the number of which would if estimated appear almost in credible; they apeared to cover several acres of ground, and were no doubt engaged in procuring their ordinary food; which is fish, on our approach they flew and left behind them several small fish of about eight inches in length, none of which I had seen before—

One of the men, Joseph Whitehouse, estimated up to six thousand pelicans were on the island and in the sky. He also reported that Lewis shot a pelican to see how much water its pouch could hold—five gallons.

Blue Lake, which wraps around most of the park, is an oxbow lake. Throughout much of its 2,341-mile length, the Missouri is full of loops. On one day, Lewis journaled that the men went around a 30-mile-long loop and, at the end of the day, were just 1.5 miles from where they had been across the neck of the loop that morning.

Like all rivers, the Missouri periodically floods, and sometimes the floodwaters cut a new channel across the bottom of a loop, leaving the water left behind in the loop as an oxbow lake, like Blue Lake.

A full-size replica of the wooden keelboat used by the expedition in 1804 is moored at the park. The men used various methods to move the boat up the Missouri. The men walked from bow to stern on the sides of the main deck while pushing poles into the riverbed. They rowed it with oars as they stood on the deck. With ropes attached to the boat, they walked and waded ahead of it to tow it. They also tied ropes to trees on the riverbanks ahead of the boat, and then stood on the boat to pull it forward. A square sail could be raised on the thirty-two-foot-high mast to catch favorable winds. The men preferred poling the keelboat.

Until 1819, when steamboats appeared on the Missouri, manpower was the only way to take a boat upriver, and some keelboats remained in use until the 1850s on waterways too shallow for the steamboats.

The Lewis and Clark keelboat was built near Pittsburgh, Pennsylvania. It was brought down the Ohio River and then up the Mississippi to near St. Louis, where the expedition was training and being outfitted. There, Lewis and Clark modified the boat for their upcoming trip, which began in May

1804. The vessel was fifty-five feet long, a bit more than eight feet wide and had a cabin at the rear. Storage lockers lined each side of the deck, and their lids could be raised to become bulwarks to provide protection for the men should they come under attack, which never happened. A small cannon on a swivel mount was at the bow. Generally, only Lewis and Clark slept on the boat.

Able to carry twelve to fourteen tons of cargo in the lockers, the eleven-ton boat went with the expedition to present-day Mandan, North Dakota. After the Corps of Discovery, which was the official name of the expedition, wintered near the Mandan and Hidatsa villages, twenty-six men were selected to return the keelboat to St. Louis, carrying items collected by the corps on the way north as well as their journals. Among the articles was a live prairie dog that Lewis was sending to President Thomas Jefferson as a gift. No record exists of what happened to the boat after it returned to St. Louis. Some speculate it may have been used by others and eventually broken up.

The replica was built by Butch Bouvier, a Council Bluffs boatwright, who was helped by Nathan Butler. During the warm months, it's docked in the water, and in the winter, it rests on a boat trailer and covered. It has an engine and propeller so it can move around Blue Lake during various events—the largest of which is Lewis and Clark Days, which occurs early every June at the park.

Another replica made in 1985 is in the large visitor center that overlooks the dock. It starred in the 1997 PBS show *Undaunted Courage* about the expedition. The center also holds replicas of two long slim boats called pirogues. Like the originals, one is painted red, the other white. Similar to the keelboat, the original pirogues could be rowed, poled, towed or sailed. Each held up to nine tons of supplies to augment what the keelboat carried. The pirogues were taken as far up the Missouri as present-day Great Falls, Montana. There, they were stored to be used on the Corps' return trip. Unfortunately, when the men came back months later, the red pirogue had been wrecked by a flood. The men then used the white pirogue and several dugout canoes to return to St. Louis in 1806.

The expedition had a fifth boat, and a copy is in the visitor center. It's the only full-size replica known to exist of the iron boat designed by Lewis. Basically a prefabricated boat that was to be carried unassembled, the boat's framework consisted of flat iron bars that had been made in Virginia and were to be screwed together when needed. Lewis planned to cover the 82-piece, 176-pound frame with hides acquired along the route, bind them to one another and the frame and then waterproof all using pitch made from tree resin.

A replica of the keelboat used by explorers Lewis and Clark floats on Blue Lake, which was once part of the Missouri River, at Lewis and Clark State Park.

However, when Lewis decided the boat should be assembled, the men were at Great Falls, a place with few trees to make pitch. The men tried a mix of bear fat, beeswax and charcoal as a substitute, but the hides fell apart, as did the plans to use the boat, which was then disassembled. Its iron pieces were stored at Great Falls, where they were recovered on the corps' return trip in 1806. Some people speculate that the iron was salvaged and used by the group's blacksmith to fashion items needed by the men and for trading with Native Americans.

HARRISON COUNTY

Murray Hill

Murray Hill provides one of the best overlooks of the Loess Hills and the valley of the Missouri River. Take Highway F20 out of Little Sioux to the east and watch for the gravel parking lot immediately ascending a slope

Common to the Loess Hills, a yucca plant blooms on Murray Hill which overlooks the Missouri River floodplain east of Little Sioux.

going north and a curve to the east. The hike up the hill from the parking lot is deceptive. At first, people think they will be at the top at the first rise they see, but when they reach there, they see another rise and then another and so on. It's not a hard hike, just deceptive.

MANNING

Manning Hausbarn Heritage Park

From about 1850 to the 1970s, Germans were the largest group of immigrants in Iowa. In 1990, half of all Iowans were descendants of the Germans who settled across the state.

Manning was no exception. Founded in 1881 at the junction of two railroads by O.H. Manning, a railroad agent, attorney and later a lieutenant governor, the new town was predominantly German.

To celebrate their German heritage, in the 1980s, residents of Manning began the process of importing a hausbarn in Schleswig-Holstein—the northernmost state in Germany and original home of many Manning immigrants—and bringing it to Manning. As the name says, the structure is a combination house and barn that was popular in Schleswig-Holstein.

One, built in 1660, was located, and luckily its owner wanted rid of it. It was disassembled and brought to Manning in pieces that were reassembled in the 1990s by locals aided by Germans who thatched the roof. About 95 percent of the rebuilt Hausbarn is its original materials.

Inside, the haus was bricked off from the rest of the building and covered less than a quarter of the floorspace.

The hausbarn is east of Manning along Iowa Highway 141 in the Manning Hausbarn Heritage Park, which also has a 1910-era homestead with a Craftsman-style bungalow and various farm buildings. The park's Trinity Church was built eleven miles away in 1913 and moved here in 2006; it is now a popular spot for weddings.

Built in 1660 in Germany, this combination house and barn was rebuilt at Manning to honor the heritage of Germans who immigrated to Iowa.

MISSOURI VALLEY

DeSoto National Wildlife Refuge

National wildlife refuges are set up for wildlife, but DeSoto National Wildlife Refuge, about six miles west of I-29 and Missouri Valley on U.S. 30, has something no other refuge has—the cargo of a sunken steamboat. On the afternoon of April 1, 1865, the sternwheeler *Bertrand* hit a snag in the Missouri River here. Although the boat sank in ten minutes, its crew and passengers safely made shore. About a third of the cargo was estimated to be salvaged within a few days, as was its propulsion machinery. Another salvage effort in 1896 recovered little more. Rumors swirled like the muddy waters with tales of valuable whiskey and mercury remaining to be found, but no whiskey and only nine wrought-iron containers of mercury were ever found, out of five hundred reportedly on the boat when it sank.

In 1965, the boat was located once more. What was left of it was found forty-five feet below the surface of a field, as the Missouri had shifted its channel over the years. More than half a million recovered artifacts, protected from the decaying effects of oxygen by the mud that had settled around them, are displayed in a climate-controlled room at the refuge's visitor center. They represent the nation's largest collection of Civil War–era items. Many are pristine.

Built in Wheeling, West Virginia, in 1864 and at a cost of $50,000, the flat-bottomed *Bertrand* was 161 feet long and 32 feet wide, and sat about 22 inches in the water when loaded. Cargo, wood for fuel and the boat's boilers were on the main deck. Some cargo was carried below that deck in the hold. The second deck held crew cabins, staterooms for passengers, a saloon and a dining room. Skylights in the ceiling of the second deck admitted light into the rooms. The third deck supported the pilot house. Passenger fares were about $150 for a one-way, usually monotonous trip between St. Louis and Fort Benton, Montana Territory, which, at two thousand miles away, was the farthest the steamboats could travel then.

On March 18, the *Bertrand* departed St. Louis for Fort Benton, the hub of materials entering and leaving a region where a gold rush was on. The time to travel the Missouri was in the spring and early summer when waters ran high with the runoff from the distant Rocky Mountains.

Goods recovered from the *Bertrand* range from the utilitarian to the fancy: bottles filled with bourbon, whiskey, wine, brandy and medicine; clothing

Thousands of artifacts, most in pristine condition, from a Missouri River paddle wheeler that sank in 1865, are in a climate-controlled room at DeSoto National Wildlife Refuge.

such as gloves, vests, dress boots, work boots, coats, dresses and hats; mirrors, silverware, platters, elegant and colorful kerosene lamps, fancy glass salt and pepper shakers, irons and clocks for houses; mustard and olive oil from France; toys; and, for the miners, shovels, picks, explosives, blacksmith tools and wrought-iron tubes of mercury (used in separating gold from other minerals). Foods in hundreds of cans and bottles included strawberries, brandied cherries, peaches, peanuts, dried beef, pork and mutton, plum tomatoes, oysters and bitters. Tests performed on some of the recovered foods showed that they were safe to eat—although they did not appear or smell appetizing.

If the *Bertrand* had made the four-month round trip, it more than likely would have returned like the steamboat *Yellowstone* did that same year with passengers, $250,000 in gold and three thousand buffalo robes. In September 1866, the *Louella* carried $1.25 million in gold, the largest haul that ever came down the Missouri. Some riverboats, which could cost up to $75,000 to build, could be paid off in one return trip. Valuable items weren't carried only going back to St. Louis. A one-hundred-pound bag of flour cost $150 (more than $2,300 in today's economy) in Fort Benton. Other foodstuffs were just as expensive. The boats also carried the mail, which, to some, was better than anything gold and flour could buy. In either direction, the steamboats were treasure ships.

Traveling on the Missouri River could be perilous. Some boats lasted just four or five years. The steamer *Western* ran for nine years, making nine round trips to Fort Benton. However, *Cora II* and *A.E. Stanard* also fell victim to snags and sank near the *Bertrand* not long after it went under. Sand sucked into the engines with cooling water ruined them. Some boats grounded on the ever-changing sandbars, and passengers were enlisted to help free them. One riverboat captain wrote of having to wait for a buffalo herd to cross a river he was traveling. Boats had to stop at times so the crew could go ashore to chop down trees or break up dead ones for firewood. Boilers blew up, dooming boats, cargo and crew. Floating ice crushed hulls.

The Nez Perce attacked the steamboat *Benton* during one trip. Twice, the boat hit snags and sank but was raised each time. Then it backed into a piling at Sioux City, which put a hole in its hull. That allowed it to drift under a nearby lowered drawbridge and tore off the upper parts of the boat. This time, when the *Benton* sank, it went down forever.

The peak of riverboat travel on the Missouri came in 1858, when about sixty large steamboats and forty to fifty smaller ones were in use. With railroads penetrating the distant reaches of the Midwest beginning in the 1870s, river travel became less and less. By the time the last steamboats worked the river around 1900, about three hundred had sunk in the Missouri.

MOORHEAD

Ingemann Danish Lutheran Church

Built in 1884 by immigrants from Denmark, Ingemann Danish Lutheran Church is one of the more picturesque historical churches in the Loess Hills. Sited on the side of a hill with a cemetery out front, the church was active until 1954. Still, it has a service on Memorial Day and is used for reunions and weddings. Unfortunately, the church was heavily vandalized in 2015, resulting in the erection of a security fence around the property. Nevertheless, the church is open during daylight hours.

To reach the church, drive less than five miles west of Moorhead on County Highway E54.

Built in 1884 by immigrants to the Loess Hills near Moorhead, the Ingemann Danish Lutheran Church was used by congregations until 1954.

PISGAH

Loess Hills State Forest Visitor Center

The Loess Hills State Forest Visitor Center is on the west edge of Pisgah, a bit more than four miles east of Murray Hill. Murals, a three-dimensional terrain model, photos and displays explain the history of the Loess Hills.

3

SOUTHWEST IOWA

ADAIR

Jesse James Train Robbery Site

The first train robbery took place in October 1866, when robbers who had boarded a train in Seymour, Indiana, looted a safe they had broken open and, unable to open another, shoved it outside the train to work on it later.

However, notorious outlaw Jesse James and up to six others of his gang made the first robbery of a moving train on July 21, 1873, near Adair, Iowa. Believing $75,000 in gold to be on an eastbound train, the men loosened a rail on the tracks of the Chicago, Rock Island and Pacific Railroad and tied a rope to it. When they saw a train approaching about 8:30 p.m., they pulled the rail out of place, and the engine toppled onto its side, killing the engineer and mortally wounding the fireman. Even though the seven passenger cars and sleepers remained upright, some passengers were injured.

Forcing a guard to open the safe on the train, the gang found only $2,000. Upset, they robbed the passengers of another $1,000 in cash and valuables and took off. Posses of armed men failed to apprehend the outlaws.

A large locomotive wheel near a section of railroad track marks the scene of the fatal robbery, less than two miles southwest of Adair on County Highway G30.

CLARINDA

Glenn Miller Boyhood Home and Museum

Glenn Miller's name will forever be linked with the swing and jazz music of the big band era from about 1910 through the 1940s. What constitutes a big band? It's a group of ten or more musicians playing saxophones, trumpets, trombones and rhythm, usually in the form of piano, bass, drums and guitars.

The Glenn Miller Boyhood Home is where the musician lived the first four years of his life. It has been restored to its appearance in 1904, the year he was born. Along with early twentieth-century furnishings, the house has items relating to Miller, including a piano he and his wife, Helen, owned, a copy of one of his gold records and photos of various events involving him, including the two movies he made.

More memorabilia may be found at the museum just behind the house. Greeting visitors inside the front door is a statue of Miller holding a trombone and wearing the uniform he wore with his orchestra members when performing for troops in distant lands during World War II. His actual trombone is in the main display gallery of the museum, as is a bandstand that was set up wherever the orchestra performed.

The second full weekend in June, Clarinda hosts the annual Glenn Miller Festival. Bands that play the big band sounds have come from across the United States and around the world—including Japan, Switzerland and the Netherlands—to play in the festival. Concerts are held in various venues in the city.

Clarinda maintains the boyhood home of musician, composer and band leader Glenn Miller as it was when he was born here in 1904.

Goldenrod School

Around the beginning of the twentieth century, a movement began in different places in the United States to educate rural youth about advances in agriculture technology. Goldenrod School was one of those places. Built in 1873 in Fremont Township, the twenty-three-by-thirty-three-foot wooden school was originally eight miles northwest of Clarinda. In 1901, twenty-year-old teacher Jessie Field began after-school clubs for students that proved to be very popular. At the time, Field designed a pin for her students to wear. Shaped as a three-leaf clover, the H on each leaf represented Hands, Head and Heart. Later, a fourth leaf was added for Health.

What Field started in Goldenrod was one part of the creation of 4-H—Ohio also claims that 4-H started there. The different programs coalesced, and now 4-H has six million members between the ages of eight and eighteen in the United States and approximately another million in fifty other countries.

Field, who is called the "Mother of 4-H," became superintendent of the 130 country schools in Page County in 1906 and wrote books to train rural

Considered by many to be the birthplace of 4-H, Goldenrod School was a one-room country schoolhouse that's now in a museum park in Clarinda.

teachers. In 1912, she moved to New York City to work with the national YMCA and YWCA organizations.

Goldenrod School was about to be torn down when, in 1965, it was moved to the grounds of the Nodaway Valley Museum on the south side of Clarinda, where it was restored to its appearance when Field taught there.

Goldenrod easily represents any of the 190,000 one-room schoolhouses that were in use in 1919 across the nation. A potbellied stove, fed with coal or wood, provided heat in the winter. The restroom was an outhouse. A hand pump provided water. One teacher taught all the students, ranging from first to eighth grade and numbering from around six to forty, in each school. Students in the early grades sat near the front of the classroom. The older students helped the younger ones learn arithmetic, reading, writing, geography and history.

In the early twentieth century, Iowa had about 14,000 one-room schoolhouses. Of those, 2,800 still exist, although none are schools. Some have become houses, storage spaces or museums, such as Goldenrod.

MILLS COUNTY

Salem Lutheran Church

Salem Lutheran Church was built in the countryside of Mills County by German immigrants in 1867. An 1870s cemetery is across the road from the church.

Built in 1867, Salem Lutheran Church is among the older buildings in Mills County and is also one of the oldest Lutheran church buildings in Iowa although its congregation left in 1933. The church was built with locally made brick and other materials that steamboats brought up the Missouri River. In 1900, the brick walls were covered with concrete. After being neglected for many years, the church—called Kirche by its first members, who were German immigrants—was rebuilt in the 1950s with another more complete restoration occurring in 2001. The wooden pews are original, as are the 1877 kerosene chandelier and crucifix.

Across the county road is an 1870s cemetery. One service is held at the church each year, at 10:00 a.m. on Memorial Day. Salem Lutheran Church is open for visits daily. The address is 50307 Ashton Road | Glenwood, Iowa.

GREENFIELD

Iowa Aviation Museum and Hall of Fame

The Iowa Aviation Museum and Hall of Fame is located in a modern hangar at the Greenfield Municipal Airport, about a mile north of town. Most of the aircraft here relate to civil aviation from 1928 to 1968. An A-7 attack bomber and an AH-1 Huey Cobra gunship, both used from Vietnam through Operation Desert Storm, stand outside the hangar, representing the U.S. military.

The hangar holds a collection of classic powered aircraft and gliders. Among the aircraft are a 1928 Curtiss Robin, a high-wing monoplane; a 1941 de Havilland Tiger Moth, which was used as a trainer by Great Britain, Canada, Australia and New Zealand during World War II; and a 1929 Northrup Primary Glider, a spindly one-seat airframe made of wire, wood and cloth that looks like it could never fly, but it did. Another aircraft is a beautiful blue and yellow 1941 Aetna-Timm 2AS, a two-seat aircraft built in hopes of becoming a trainer used by the U.S. military, but another firm won the contract—this is the only one left of six built. A 1929 Stearman biplane that once flew for Tri-State Airlines between Omaha, Sioux City and Minneapolis is here along with a 1946 Taylorcraft, a Pitts Special S2S that dominated aerobatic competitions for decades after World War II, and a Piper J-2, a type that was flown primarily by private airplane owners.

The Hall of Fame includes Iowans John Livingston, the leading winner of air races across the nation in the 1920s and 1930s; three members of Doolittle's Raiders; George "Bud" Day, who won the Medal of Honor and survived five and a half years as a POW during the Vietnam War; astronaut Dr. Peggy W. Whitson, who flew on the space shuttle and was the first female to command the International Space Station; Lieutenant General Charles Horner, commander of U.S. and Allied air forces during Desert Storm; and Ann Pellegreno, who, in 1967, successfully flew the route Amelia Earhart had failed to complete thirty years earlier.

A family looks at one of the many historic and rare aircraft at the Iowa Museum and Hall of Fame at the Greenfield Airport.

A room contains several aviation artifacts. Watch the museum's calendar for its annual fly-in breakfast, when many pilots from around the region bring their personal aircraft to Greenfield.

MOUNT AYR

U.S. Post Office

The mural inside the Mount Ayr Post Office is representative of many oil-on-canvas paintings made from 1934 to 1943 to place in the lobbies of post offices in 1,300 cities across the United States. They were part of a competitive art program administered by the U.S. Department of the Treasury. Called New Deal Art, it sometimes is mistaken for art administered the Works Project Administration. The paintings, averaging five feet high by twelve feet wide, were chosen to be put in post offices since those were the most frequently visited government buildings in most communities. The competing artists were told to avoid controversial subjects and to be representative of the region near each post office. Of the 850 artists selected for the program, 162 were women and 3 were African American.

Ora C. Fisher painted Mount Ayr's colorful vibrant *Corn on Parade* mural in 1941. Other Iowa post offices that participated in the program were Ames, Audubon, Bloomfield, Clarion, Columbus Junction, Corning, Cresco, DeWitt, Dubuque (two), Emmetsburg, Forest City, Harlan, Hawarden, Ida Grove, Independence, Jefferson, Knoxville, Leon, Manchester, Marion, Missouri Valley, Monticello, Mount Pleasant (two), New Hampton, Onawa, Osceola, Pella, Rockwell City, Sigourney, Tipton and Waverly.

TABOR

Todd House

John Todd left his native Pennsylvania in 1835 to study at what is now Ohio's Oberlin College, which was then a hot spot for antislavery activists. After graduating from there and then a seminary, he became a Congregational minister in 1844. However, his first congregation in Ohio wasn't as fervent

A foe of slavery, John Todd built his home in the pre–Civil War years in Tabor to shelter slaves seeking freedom on the Underground Railroad.

about abolition as he was. So, at a friend's invitation, he and some followers settled in Tabor in 1852.

Todd built a simple-looking two-story home for his family there the next year, but it was more than that. It was a station on the Underground Railroad for runaway slaves heading north to freedom. Some say Todd and others in Tabor helped several hundred former slaves on their way to freedom. "Conductors" from the town helped guide the runaways to the next stops.

Todd's house was also a rest for "Free Staters," abolitionists heading to Kansas, a battleground between proslavery and antislavery forces from 1854 to 1861. Some of the men used the park across the street from the house as their camp and for training.

Ammunition, weapons and clothing were stored in the basement for abolitionist forces—so were fleeing slaves at times. Some were also secreted in a small upstairs area that was accessible by a hidden stairway from the first floor.

In early 1859, arch-abolitionist John Brown arrived in town for a few days with a group of his supporters and twelve former slaves they had freed in Missouri. On a Sunday, Brown was about to deliver a talk in a church when he realized a proslavery physician from Missouri was among the listeners. Rather than say anything more, he left the assembly. However, afterward, his supporters engaged in conversations with supporters of the Missouri physician, each side using biblical passages to justify their positions.

Brown briefly stopped in Tabor one more time, in September 1859, to visit a friend. More than a month later, he led a party of abolitionists, many carrying arms that had been stored in Tabor, in an abortive attempt to seize the federal arsenal at Harpers Ferry, Virginia. The Reverend Todd said while he knew that Brown and his men had taken the weapons, he had no knowledge they were going to be used at Harpers Ferry.

VILLISCA

Villisca Axe Murder House

On a typical weekday morning, like the one of June 11, 1912, in Villisca, Iowa, which then had a population of 2,039, most people were busy with chores or going to work. So, when sixty-three-year-old Mary Peckham saw no one moving around her neighbor's house at 7:30 a.m., she thought it strange. The sun had been up for nearly two hours on this midsummer day.

Wondering, she knocked at the door of Josiah and Sarah Moore's house, but no one answered. Peckham called Josiah's brother Ross, who brought along a key to the front door.

Telling Peckham to wait, he went inside. In a first-floor bedroom, he saw two figures covered with sheets and blood on the bed frame. Stopping there, he called for Peckham to fetch the town marshal.

In not much time, word was out across town: Josiah, forty-three, and Sarah, thirty-nine, plus their four children, ages five to eleven, and two young girlfriends of one of their daughters were dead, murdered. The blunt end of an axe head had been used to kill everyone except Josiah, who had been struck repeatedly with the axe blade. The axe, almost wiped clean, leaned against a bedroom wall. Bloodhounds followed a scent to the nearby Nodaway River, where it disappeared.

The news sent not only the town but also the nation reeling. The *New York Times* printed the story the next morning. Murders like this just did not happen in 1912.

One suspect was questioned six days later but let go when authorities learned he had been almost across the state on the night of the murders. As time went on, fears mounted and theories flew. Some said a business competitor of Josiah's did it. Others thought a man suspected of multiple

An unidentified assailant killed eight people with an axe in this home in Villisca on the night of June 10, 1912. No one was convicted of the murders.

murders, some done with an axe, in Illinois and Colorado was the culprit, but his alibi checked out.

Then suspicion fell on the Reverend George Kelly, a traveling minister who had been in Villisca that weekend and left on a train just before sunrise on the morning the bodies were found. Kelly was arrested in 1917 on a charge of murder and went through two trials that year. The first trial ended with a hung jury, and he was acquitted in the second.

No one ever was found guilty of the murders.

The house has been restored to how it appeared when the Moores lived there. Daytime tours are given, and with arrangements, some can stay overnight. Ghost hunters and paranormal seekers have visited the house, many coming up with their own theories of who murdered eight people in June 1912.

The axe is in safekeeping in Villisca.

THE SODA FOUNTAINS OF SOUTHWEST IOWA

Although no one has possibly researched that the soda fountains of southwest Iowa have spawned more romantic relationships than the Bridges of Madison County, one might be able to safely place bets on the soda fountains.

The sweet spot in the history of soda fountains lasted from early in the twentieth century through the 1960s. Nearly every town in America had a pharmacy, and almost every pharmacy had a soda fountain where customers could cool their heels and tongues while waiting for their prescriptions to be filled. Spoons were made small—so customers would take smaller bites and linger longer in the stores—and long to reach deep into chilled glasses that held sodas, ice creams, sundaes, milkshakes, malts and phosphates made tingly with flavored carbonated waters.

Behind the counters were buckets of hard ice cream, sometimes homemade. Gleaming Hamilton Beach mixers whirred, turning ice cream into shakes and malts. Shiny chrome lids covered cherry and strawberry sauces and pineapple, chocolate, butterscotch and hot fudge toppings that were ladled over mounds of ice cream. Real whipped cream topped many treats, including banana splits.

Nicknames abounded. A Green River was a carbonated lime-based soda with a touch of lemon. A Brown Cow was a root beer float made with chocolate ice cream. Combining all the flavors of the phosphates available at a soda fountain was called a Suicide. The employees who doled out the ice cream and made the wonderful treats were called soda jerks. Some joked they were fizzisians.

The emergence of fast foods, self-service drugstores, cans and bottles of soda pop and commercially made ice creams that people could take home spelled the end for most soda fountains. Many pharmacies tore out their soda fountains, replacing them with more profitable items, including over-the-counter medicines, foot powders, hairbrushes, makeup, small groceries and photo frames.

Even though, by comparison to all those items weighing down the shelves, soda fountains might be thought of as money losers, there's something to be said about retaining nostalgia in the form of the sweetest, coldest concoctions people have ever tasted.

Once, perhaps thousands of soda fountains were pumping sweet treats across the United States. No one knows exactly how many are left. In Iowa, the guess is between one and two dozen are still tantalizing the tongues of all ages.

Sidney: Penn Drug

Located on the west side of the courthouse square in downtown Sidney (population 1,037), Penn Drug is the oldest family-run pharmacy in Iowa, opening in 1860. The original owner left town in 1863, some say to fight for the Union in the Civil War, and sold his business to Dr. John Newton Penn, a physician who had arrived in 1855. Upon buying the predecessor's stock of drugs, Penn built his new business facing the courthouse on the square. The store was on the first floor, and his medical office was on a balcony at the rear of the first floor. The pharmacy, on one side of the first floor, was where the medicines were mixed. In those years, practically all medicines were compounded by hand.

Smiles come free with cold treats served at the soda fountain in Penn Drug in Sidney. Southwest Iowa has a number of old-time soda fountains.

Penn's son, Alphonso, took over the pharmacy and installed a soda fountain in 1898. That was replaced in the 1920s by one with a marble countertop. That one gave way to another, the present one, in 1947, when a few food items for lunch were added to the menu. Gifts and cards were added to the store, too, but after the pharmacy, the heart of the business in the eyes and taste buds of many who have been here is the soda fountain. Visitors sit on the ten cushion-topped stools in front of the counter where they can watch dreams get made right in front of them. Four tables also offer seating. In 2015, the business was sold to Angie Ettleman (who has worked there for thirty-plus years), her husband, Leo, and business partner Mark Vogt, although they have kept the name Penn Drug.

Corning: McMahon Drug

For several years, the town of Corning was blessed with two soda fountains a few doors from each other on the town's main street. When Getter's Pharmacy was open, people went there to drink Pepsi. For Coca-Cola, they visited McMahon Drug, which is now operated by HyVee Inc., a large grocery retailer in the Midwest. In the past, visiting kids would mix as many flavors as they could such as a grape/orange/Seven-Up to see what they could stomach…or not. Finally, the owners limited the young visitors to two self-serve flavors per drink.

Hamburg: Stoner Drug Company

Stoner Drug Company's name comes from founder Oscar Stoner, who opened the business in 1896, way before *stoner* became associated with a person overly fond of illegal drugs. When the store moved to its present location in 1956, the 1927 marble-face soda fountain came along with everything else. That was a good thing for lovers of antique soda fountains. Stoner Drug owns five pharmacies in southwest Iowa, northwest Missouri and southeast Nebraska, but this is the only one with a soda fountain.

Shenandoah: George Jay Drug

George Jay Drug has been a fixture on the main drag through Shenandoah's downtown since George Jay Sr. built it in 1888. The store installed a soda fountain a few years later, and that was replaced in 1938 by the one where people are bellying up to the counter today. Cherry Cokes are mixed by hand, not poured from a can or bottle. The soda jerks say it's not a secret about the malt powder they use—it's sold in any grocery. But knowing how much to use to make a malt takes practice. An enormous brass cash register sits at the back bar, another item recalling the heyday of soda fountains.

4

NORTH-CENTRAL IOWA

CHARLES CITY

Carrie Lane Chapman Catt Girlhood Home

Through the latter years of the nineteenth century and into the twentieth, Carrie Chapman Catt was a well-known national leader in the efforts to pass the Nineteenth Amendment guaranteeing women's right to vote. When she was seven years old, in 1866, she moved with her family from Wisconsin into this two-story brick farmhouse built by her father about three miles south of Charles City. At the age of thirteen, she asked why her mother was not voting in an election and was told that voting was too important for women.

That day, Catt later told others, was when she resolved to get women the right to vote. After high school, she was the only woman in her class to graduate from what later became Iowa State University. Then came a long series of working with different women's organizations, delivering public speeches, writing articles about the importance of women, dealing with male politicians who she thought didn't care about women's rights and traveling across the states to establish suffrage organizations. In 1900, she was elected president of the National Woman Suffrage Association on the strength of her relentless organizational skills. She was also known for working with different factions in women's organizations to get them to work on common causes. In 1904, she became president of the International Woman Suffrage Association, which helped to establish similar organizations in thirty-two countries, many of which she visited to help their causes.

Carrie Lane Chapman Catt, who worked ceaselessly for women's rights, lived in this house built by her father near Charles City in 1866.

Catt married twice. Leo Chapman died the year after they married in 1885. In 1890, she married George Catt, who supported her cause and financially helped her efforts until he died in 1915.

In 1920, the Nineteenth Amendment was passed, giving women the right to vote.

Afterward, Catt pressed for international disarmament, supported the League of Nations, was instrumental in forming the League of Women Voters, helped child labor protection laws and worked for the relief of Jewish refugees. In 1921, she became the first woman to address a commencement at Iowa State University.

Catt died in 1947 in New Rochelle, New York, where she had lived for many years.

CLEAR LAKE

Surf Ballroom

Dance halls were so popular during the early part of the twentieth century that many towns had one. Clear Lake's was the Surf Ballroom, which opened in 1934 on the lake's northeast shore. It was named the Surf because owner Carl Fox imagined is as an oceanside dance club. Hand-painted murals of wave-kissed sandy beaches, palm trees and sailboats adorned the interior walls. Besides the first levels' dance floor, a roof garden was upstairs for dancing outside. Faux palm trees stood on the stage. Big band and swing music was popular in the 1930s and 1940s, and those who played at the Surf included Duke Ellington, Glenn Miller, Lawrence Welk, Tommy Dorsey and Benny Goodman.

In 1947, the Surf burned down, and the new owners built a larger one across the street. They maintained the Surf's theme and had stars projected on the dark ceiling to make the dancers feel they were outdoors. Covering 30,000 square feet, the new Surf held up to 2,100 people dancing on the 6,300-square-foot hardwood floor or sitting in about one hundred booths along two sides of the dance floor.

When the sounds of the big bands slowly gave way to the shock waves of rock 'n' roll, the owners of the Surf adapted to the new reverberations, bringing Jerry Lee Lewis, Roy Orbison, the Everly Brothers, Little Richard, Bill Haley and others to the cavernous ballroom.

In January 1959, a group of possibly the top rockers in the nation started a twenty-four-day tour that would take them to twenty-four cities across the Midwest. Headlining the tour was Buddy Holly, who had been turning out hits since releasing "That Will Be the Day" in May 1957. Because he had just split with the Crickets, Holly picked up Waylon Jennings to play bass, Tommy Allsup on guitar and Carl Bunch on drums.

Others on the tour were Dion and the Belmonts and Frankie Sardo. The musicians started their "Winter Party Tour" on January 23 in Milwaukee and traveled through severely cold weather after each performance to the next stop, sometimes hundreds of miles away, while riding in an unheated bus that often had other problems. In the dark early hours of February 1, the bus engine gave out, stranding the musicians near Hurley, Wisconsin, for a while. Later that day, Bunch was hospitalized for frostbitten feet he suffered while in the cold bus. Valens and Richardson felt like they were catching the flu. Others were grumpy and tired of traveling like this, trying to sleep while sitting in the bus. Holly told someone it was the tour from hell.

On the evening of February 2, a day that started at thirteen degrees below zero, the tour arrived at the Surf shortly before the show was to open at 8:00 p.m. after having driven 350 miles. Before going on stage, Holly arranged with Richard Dwyer, a pilot and owner of a flying service at the nearby Mason City Airport, to set up a post-concert flight to the tour's next stop at Moorhead, Minnesota. The Beechcraft 35 Bonanza could carry three passengers in addition to the pilot.

The Surf Ballroom was where rockers Buddy Holly, J.P. "The Big Bopper" Richardson and Ritchie Valens played their last concert, in front of at least 1,500 people, on February 2, 1959.

That done, Holly took the stage first, playing "Gotta Travel On" in front of about 1,500 to 2,000 people. Each paid $1.25 admission.

Holly's musicians backed the other performers. With Bunch absent, Carlo Mastrangelo of the Belmonts manned the drums until it was time for Dion and the Belmonts to perform. Then Valens handled the drums for a while and next Holly sat down at them, too. Between sets, the performers visited with their fans.

Holly offered the remaining two seats on the flight to others, and it was decided that Valens and Richardson would fly. Before leaving the Surf, Holly used the backstage pay phone to talk for a few moments with his wife, Maria Elena.

A few minutes later, while the others got on the bus once more, Holly, Valens and Richardson were driven to the airport. Airport manager Dwyer wasn't there, but twenty-one-year-old pilot Roger Peterson was. He checked the weather, and the decision to fly was made. They climbed into the Bonanza, and at 12:55 a.m., Peterson lifted it into the dark sky.

Dwyer arrived at the airport at that moment and watched the taillight of the plane as it lost altitude while heading to the northwest. He radioed Peterson but never heard a reply.

About 9:30 the next morning, Dwyer took off in another plane and, using the heading that Peterson had used, found the Bonanza had crashed into a farm field just six miles from the airport. The flight had lasted no more than five minutes.

When authorities arrived at the crumpled wreck, they found the bodies of the four men. Peterson was still in the aircraft. The others had been thrown clear of it. A light snow covered their bodies.

Word of the crash spread, shocking the world of rock 'n' roll. Thanks to songwriter-performer Don McLean, February 2, 1959, became known as the "Day the Music Died." That was practically the subtitle of his real title, "American Pie," an homage to the passing of the 1950s as symbolized by the musicians' deaths. (Sometime after his 1971 song became a hit, McLean wrote part of "American Pie" on a wall in the Surf's green room, where performers can rest before and between acts. Signatures of many musicians cover its walls.)

Despite the tragedy, the other artists of the Winter Party Tour stuck to their schedule. That night, they played in the armory in Moorhead and then finished the tour at Springfield, Illinois, on February 15.

On February 2, 1979, the Surf started a Winter Dance Party to honor Holly, Richardson and Valens, and it has become a popular multiday annual event centered on February 2 that draws visitors from around the world.

Buddy Holly Crash Site

Officially, no name exists for where the Bonanza crashed about five miles north of Clear Lake. The farmer who owns the field on the south side of the site graciously allows visitors to go there. Everyone must walk closely along a field fence for about a third of a mile west of the intersection of 315th Street and Gull Avenue to where the plane crashed. An overly large pair of black-frame glasses—resembling those Holly wore—marks the intersection.

Ken Paquette, of Porterfield, Wisconsin, built a stainless-steel monument featuring a guitar and three records bearing the names of the musicians' hit songs at the crash site. Later, he added another monument to honor pilot Roger Peterson. Other memorials, mostly temporary ones of flowers and mementos of the '50s and '60s, have appeared over the years.

A metal sculpture of Buddy Holly's signature black-frame eyeglasses marks the beginning of a trail that leads to where he and three others died in a nighttime airplane crash in early 1959.

FORT DODGE

The Cardiff Giant

In the fall of 1869, two workmen digging a well on William Newell's farm near Cardiff, New York, hit something solid. In a few moments, they had uncovered what looked like a large petrified foot. Soon, they were looking at the remains of a ten-foot-tall human. He was resting in the nude, one hand tucked behind his backside, the other laid across his abdomen. Word got out, and people clamored to see the petrified giant. Newell set up an exhibition tent and charged admission. Legends sprang up about the giant's origin. Ministers said it was proof that Genesis 6:4 was right when it mentioned giants were once on earth.

Named the Cardiff Giant, the petrified remains were bought by Syracuse banker David Hannum, who moved it to Syracuse to handle the growing crowds.

When showman P.T. Barnum's offer of $60,000 for the giant was refused, he hired a sculptor to make a copy for his shows and claimed it was the original. Hannum said of Barnum's bogus giant, "There's a sucker born every minute," a quote that is often misattributed to Barnum.

Finally, in late 1869, New York tobacconist George Hull confessed to having traveled to the gypsum mines near Fort Dodge in 1868 to purchase a large block of gypsum. He told the quarrymen it was for a statue of Abraham Lincoln. He then shipped the block to Chicago, where a stonecutter sworn to secrecy carved it into the shape of a large man. It was stained, and acid was poured on it to make it look old. Large needles were used to create pores in the skin. Later that year, Hull shipped the boxed sculpture east by railroad and, in league with Newell, buried it on Newell's farm. There, it "aged" for about a year before the two unsuspecting well diggers found it.

After the hoax was revealed, the giant created by Hull was exhibited with little attention in the 1901 Pan-American Exposition. It then returned to Iowa, where it was bought by a publisher to use as a coffee table. In 1947, he sold it to the Farmer's Museum in Cooperstown, New York, where it remains today.

A full-size replica is displayed at Fort Dodge's Fort Museum and Pioneer Village, which also recalls the early days of the fort and city.

MASON CITY

Birdsall's Ice Cream

Since opening in 1931, Birdsall's Ice Cream continues to serve its homemade ice cream as unadorned as could be in plain cones and dishes or as sodas, malts, shakes, splits and eight types of sundaes or mixed with bits of candy bars to become blusters.

The ice cream is made in at least twenty-two flavors and also can be served in homemade waffle cones. Stools stand around a curved part of the serving counter and tables

Historic Park Inn

When Mason City lawyer J.E.E. Markley sent his daughters to a school run by Unitarians in Spring Green, Wisconsin, he was impressed with the building's design. It was the work of a young architect who had grown up in the area, Frank Lloyd Wright. Wright was slowly upending the world of architectural design in the United States and was spearheading a movement called Prairie School Architecture that included elements such as large overhanging eaves and broad horizontal lines and being only two stories or less. It has been called the nation's first indigenous style of architecture.

Markley and his law partner, James Blythe, had wanted a new structure for their firm and hoped to augment their income by including a hotel and a bank. In 1907, they approached Wright, and he took the commission. His plans called for the bank to occupy one end of the block-long, all-brick complex. That was connected to a smaller portion that contained the law office, and that was linked on its other side to a forty-two-room hotel.

During the construction of the building that faced the main downtown city park, Wright, who was married and had six children, ran off with the wife of one of his clients. With Wright gone, his associate William Drummond saw the project through its completion in 1910. The two-story bank interior was lit by windows surrounding the second story. Skylights brought in more light. The hotel had a two-story ballroom, a ladies' parlor that adjoined a balcony overlooking the park and a men's lounge in the basement.

Mason City began to suffer economic hardships in the 1920s, and the complex designed by Wright was not exempt. The bank folded, and

A bank-hotel-office building complex designed by architect Frank Lloyd Wright in 1907 faces Mason City's main park. It is all a boutique hotel now, the Historic Park Inn.

commercial stores moved into its space. The hotel rooms became apartments. The complex gradually fell into disrepair. The hotel closed in 1972. Many elements of the Prairie School design, such as its stained-glass windows, woodwork, furniture and fixtures, were lost or misplaced. Twenty-four panels forming the stained-glass ceiling in the dining room disappeared.

Rather than watch what had been an architectural gem—it was the last surviving hotel of the six that Wright designed around the world—fade into nothing, citizens began efforts in 2000 to save the complex. Ultimately, a foundation, Wright on the Park Inc., took control of the $18 million restoration. Original materials were brought back and refurbished to their initial condition or re-created. Modern conveniences, including an elevator, were installed in the structure. The missing glass dining room ceiling panels were located in James Blythe's former home and reinstalled in the hotel.

On the exterior, the complex, renamed the Historic Park Street Inn, a boutique hotel, looks much like Wright had designed it. Guest rooms were reduced in number to twenty-seven larger ones with modern amenities. Six are in the former bank, and no two look alike. One suite is reserved as designed in 1910.

The bank lobby is now the hotel's ballroom.

Stockman House and Rock Crest—Rock Glen Historic District

During one of his visits to Mason City during the construction of the bank/law office/hotel complex, Frank Lloyd Wright met James Blythe's neighbors, George and Eleanor Stockman, who engaged him to design a house for them. Wright created what he called a "fireproof house" for the Stockmans, who lived in it from when it was built in 1908 to 1924. Then came a series of owners. Although only a few changes were made to the house, it was clearly worn down by 1987, when it was put up for auction upon the death of the last owner.

A church was about to buy it to knock it down, wanting to use its land for a parking lot. However, businessman and philanthropist David Murphy worked out a deal with the church where the house would be moved to a new location. It also ended up in the hands of River City Society for Historic Preservation, which restored the house. Only a few original items in the house remain, but it has been furnished with Arts and Crafts–style furniture and oriental rugs. Original drawings by Wright and reproductions are displayed in the house, as is gold and white china that was used in Tokyo's Imperial Hotel, also designed by Wright.

The two-story, four-bedroom house began tours in 1992. In 2011, the society opened its Mason City Architectural Interpretive Center just north of the Stockman House. Tours of the house begin in the center, which also has displays about the Prairie School style and a gift shop.

Near Stockman House is the Rock Crest–Rock Glen Historic District, the nation's largest collection of homes designed in Prairie School style; it

While in town designing the complex in downtown Mason City, Wright started the design of this house for George and Eleanor Stockman.

became popular here with the construction of the Wright's Park Inn Hotel and City National Bank complex. Designing the homes on both sides of a deep rocky gorge were William Drummond, Einar Broaten, Barry Byrne, Walter Burley Griffin (who later designed Canberra, the capital city of Australia) and his wife, Marion Mahony Griffin. Wright drew designs for a house planned to be here, but it was not built. Besides supplying information for self-guided walking tours around the exteriors of the houses, Wright on the Park Inc. offers docent-led tours of the Historic Park Inn complex and the Rock Crest–Rock Glen neighborhood.

Meredith Willson Boyhood Home

Who knew one person could have as many titles as musician Meredith Willson—composer, conductor, bandleader, playwright, radio performer and author—whose most famous works were the plays and movies *The Music Man* and *The Unsinkable Molly Brown*. Popular songs he wrote include "76 Trombones" from *The Music Man*, and "It's Beginning to Look a Lot Like Christmas," which he wrote in 1951 and was used later in his musical *Here's Love*. His song "Till There Was You," which was written for *The Music Man*, was covered by the Beatles in 1963.

He scored several movies, produced three television specials, composed symphonies and wrote three autobiographies.

Willson was born in this home in 1902 as the youngest of three children. He learned to play the piano, flute and piccolo in his early years before joining the high school marching band. At seventeen, he left Mason City with his piccolo to study music at the Damrosch Institute of Musical Art (later renamed the Juilliard School). While there, he played with John Philip Sousa's marching band. For a while, he experimented with bringing sound to movies and later moved to Hollywood to work with motion pictures. In 1951, he began laying groundwork for a musical he was creating about his early years in Mason City. At first, he called it *The Silver Triangle*, but it was renamed *The Music Man* by the time it premiered in 1957. It won eight Tony Awards, including Best Musical. In 1962, it became a hit movie. During these same years, he also wrote *The Unsinkable Molly Brown*, which opened on Broadway in 1960 and, four years later, became a movie.

Although Willson never returned to live in Mason City, he visited here several times. In 1962, he led a truly big parade of 121 high school bands from across the nation to march through the city. It was one of the events that

A statue of composer Meredith Willson stands joyous in a plaza near his childhood home.

weekend when *The Music Man* held its national premiere here. A statue of Willson leading a parade with his hat held high stands on a plaza alongside his birthplace.

Willson died in 1984 and is buried in the city's Elmwood–St. Joseph Municipal Cemetery.

Every Memorial Day weekend, the city hosts the North Iowa Band Festival, the Midwest's largest free marching band competition. It has drawn up to sixty thousand spectators.

Suzie Q

In the 1930s, Arthur Valentine of Wichita, Kansas, owner of about fifty lunchrooms in the state, became a salesman for a company that had made prefabricated diners for him. Eventually, he bought the company, and, in one of those one-thing-led-to-another stories, around 1947, he created the Valentine Manufacturing Company to make prefab sandwich shops. They could be trucked on flatbed trailers to locations in the United States and dropped off, almost ready to serve meals in a few days.

One of the four diners that Valentine delivered to Iowa in 1947 is now Suzie Q, in downtown Mason City. Over the years, its red, black and white exterior scheme has changed a bit, as have the owners and sometimes the menus, but overall, it's the same that it was when it came off the trailer in 1947. Inside, nine stools curl around a red-topped counter, and that's it for seating. At dusk, those eating here might wonder if they're reenacting artist Edward Hopper's evening painting *Nighthawks*.

Suzie Q changed hands lately, and the new owner indicates some changes to the menu might occur but says the Spic-N-Span pork tenderloin sandwich, which was judged second best in the state, will remain.

As best as is known, Valentine Manufacturing made about two hundred diners and placed them in twenty-eight states. Perhaps up to sixty remain in business as diners now, two-thirds of them in Kansas. All four diners delivered to Iowa continue to cook. The others are Dinky Diner in Decatur City, Clamshell Diner in Muscatine and Grand Diner in Spencer.

ROCKFORD

Fossil & Prairie Park Preserve

A fossil found in Rockford's Fossil & Prairie Park Preserve is a fossil that someone can keep. The preserve is one of the few places in the nation where visitors can take what they discover.

During the Devonian period around 375 million years ago, this area of the world was the floor of a large shallow sea teeming with aquatic life. When those creatures died, their remains settled on the ocean floor where, over the intervening millions of years, they were covered with layers of sediment and became fossilized.

In the late nineteenth century, the clay made of all those sediments just west of Rockford was of such high quality that a business began to quarry the area. Workers pressed the clay into molds that were fired in large kilns to make bricks. Lots of bricks. As in hundreds of millions of tons of bricks a day.

However, building contractors began using materials other than bricks as the twentieth century progressed, and the demand for bricks fell to such that the last owner, Rockford Brick & Tile Company, closed the site in 1990.

Within a year, the site was purchased to become an addition to Floyd County's thirty-two parks. Besides covering 402 acres, much of which are native prairie, this new park had something that few parks anywhere in the nation have—millions of fossils from the Devonian period. Visitors can easily find more than two hundred species of fossilized fauna and flora, and best yet, they can keep what they find, making this one of the few places in the United States that allows visitors to do that.

Thanks to erosion caused by rain, wind and melting snows, the fossils in the preserve are constantly changing. Just by flipping a small rock or scratching the sandy soil, one might claim brachiopods, crinoids, bryozoans and coral. Cephalopods, gastropods and pelecypods have also been found here. Some already may be in the open.

Beyond the quarry's fossils, the park's prairie sustains more than one hundred types of native plants along the five miles of trails that wind through the preserve. Visitors can also see three of the sixteen beehive kilns that baked clay into bricks for nearly a century. The preserve has an impressive interpretive center, a picnic shelter and information signs.

5

CENTRAL IOWA

BOONE

Boone & Scenic Valley Railroad

The first railroad in Iowa was completed between Davenport and Muscatine in November 1855. Two months later, the track was extended to Iowa City. Because no bridges crossed the Mississippi River then, the locomotive for that railroad was ferried across the river.

A wooden railroad bridge was completed across the Mississippi at Davenport in April 1856, but it was short-lived. Fifteen days after it opened, a steamboat hit the bridge, and the resulting fire destroyed the steamer and the bridge. Four months later, the bridge reopened, and railroad construction took off.

By 1867, the state was crossed from Davenport to Council Bluffs, but it wasn't until 1869 that Iowa was linked to the Transcontinental Railroad when a bridge was finally built across the Missouri. The peak number of railroad miles in Iowa came in 1917 with 10,500 miles crisscrossing the state—only three states had more tracks. No Iowan lived more than 12 miles from a railroad. At the time, railroads carried about half the freight being moved across the nation.

By the late 1940s, railroads were being used less and less with competition from aircraft. The battle for hauling freight and people grew even stiffer with the coming of the interstate highway system. By the 1970s, passenger service was almost severed except for the creation of the national rail service

The steam engine that's the pride and joy of the Boone and Scenic Valley Railroad in Boone pulls an excursion train through woods and farm fields west of town.

Amtrak. Now, Iowa has 3,905 miles of railroad tracks in operation, and Amtrak is the state's only passenger service.

To preserve the history of passenger service in Iowa, a group of railroad enthusiasts formed the Boone & Scenic Valley Railroad, using an eleven-mile-long track that had been part of an interurban rail line between Fort Dodge and the capital city, Des Moines. Now, the heritage railroad operates round-trip excursion trains between Boone and the end of the line, lunch and dinner trains and trains for special events.

Its eight diesel locomotives have a variety of histories and are painted in the colors of famous railroad companies. Some of the larger ones pull the excursion trains, while smaller engines shuttle railroad cars in the trainyard near the depot. In late 1989, the B&SVRR added another engine to its collection—the last steam locomotive made at the Datong Engine Works in China. With red-painted wheels and cowcatcher plus the U.S. and Chinese flags, this engine is used only on weekends.

Similarly, the restored passenger cars are varied: coaches, a bi-level car with seating on two floors, a concession car, dining cars used by Union Pacific Railroad on its City of Los Angeles and City of San Francisco trains, two cabooses and a small car with open-air seating.

During the excursions, the trains pass through woods, along fields and across two bridges. One passes over the Des Moines River, and another stands 154 feet above a valley floor, possibly causing some passengers to reconsider Iowa's reputation for flatness.

A trolley that was made in 1915 to run between three communities in northeast Iowa, is beautifully restored. Now, it runs round-trips from the depot to downtown Boone, a half-mile away.

Built to look like a 1900 depot, the B&SVRR's main building is the ticket office and waiting room. A nine-thousand-square-foot museum full of railroad history and artifacts is next to the depot.

COLO

Reed/Niland Corner

With the coming of the Lincoln Highway in 1913 and, in 1916, the Jefferson Highway, the first north–south highway in the United States from Canada to New Orleans, Charlie Reed and his nephew Clare Niland thought to take advantage of the traffic that would be passing through the intersection of those highways. It didn't hurt that Reed's farmland abutted the intersection's northwest corner.

In 1923, Reed opened a gas station there, selling gasoline for less than eighteen cents a gallon. Then the Niland family opened a small lunch stand at another location. After it grew, it was moved nearer to the gas station and named the L&J Café. The service station and café were open 24/7. Sometimes, people stopping at the gas station and café camped on their lawn.

Seeing another way to help travelers, Reed added cabins, a restroom-shower building for guests staying in the cabins and, later, a motel that would expand over the years. An apartment house also was built. Two long-distance bus lines stopped here to let their passengers and drivers grab a bite. The café was known for good cooking, and the ham and bean soup was its signature item.

The area became called the Reed/Niland Corner. It was the first one-stop business on the Lincoln Highway in Iowa and was a forerunner of the service plazas that were built in decades to come along other highways.

The U.S. government gave the highways numbers. In 1926, the Lincoln Highway became U.S. 30. The Jefferson became U.S. 65. They had crisscrossed on level ground in Y intersections near the Reed/Niland Corner until a bridge was built to carry U.S. 30 over U.S. 65. U.S. 30 was eventually moved a mile to the south, and the old highway's designation became County Road E41, although it's still the Lincoln Highway to most folks here.

The number of motorists traveling through here fell over the years. The gas station closed in 1967 and the café in 1991. The other buildings, except for the apartments, closed in 1995. Then private citizens and the Colo Development Group worked to bring the corner back to life. The café and station were restored in 2004. Four years later, the motel was substantially renovated. Five rooms are available for overnight guests.

Some claim the corner is the best-preserved one-stop remaining on the Lincoln Highway in Iowa. Known by the name it was given in the 1930s,

Niland's Café, it is open 7:00 a.m. to 8:00 p.m. Tuesday through Saturday and from 7:00 a.m. to 2:00 p.m. Sunday for brunch. The front third of a 1939 Cadillac juts into the dining room from a corner. Diners sit in booths, at tables and on stools lining the counter. The food, from eggs in the morning to pies in the evening, is homemade, and ham and bean soup is still on the stove.

The gas station is now a museum featuring mostly equipment and tools that had been used there for decades. One quirky item in the station's office is a deer foot that was to be used as a club to ward off would-be robbers. (No one knows if it was ever used.) Bright-red gas pumps, which once dispensed Red Crown Gasoline, stand tall between the brown brick columns holding up the overhang that sheltered motorists from the rain.

DES MOINES METRO AREA (INCLUDES WEST DES MOINES, URBANDALE AND WINDSOR HEIGHTS)

What's in a Name?

When it comes down to it, the city of Des Moines was, in a roundabout way, named after the Des Moines River, which flows through Iowa's capital city after starting in southwest Minnesota and ending at the Mississippi River near the town of Keokuk.

The French were the first Europeans to see Iowa. On June 25, 1673, explorers Louis Jolliet and Father Jacques Marquette set foot on the west side of the Mississippi near where the Des Moines River empties into it. Walking to the west, they found a village occupied by Peolaualen (later Peoria) and another by Moingona. Both spoke dialects of the Algonquian language shared by many Native Americans in the region. Although a 1718 French map had the river named "le Moingona R.," and another map had "des Moines ou le Moigona" river, most maps used "La Rivière des Moines" or in English, the Des Moines River.

Some people later took the last variation to mean "River of the Monks," but no monks were known to be in the area. Some say that Moin, Moine and Moines were alternative references to Moingona, meaning "Clan of the Loon," or "People by the Portage," referring to the village near the mouth of the Des Moines River. Also, a dictionary of translations between French and regional Native American words of the late seventeenth century by a Jesuit suggest that Moin was how the Indians who met French referred to some upriver Indians in a derogatory manner.

Besides naming the waterway the Des Moines River on their maps, Americans gave the name Fort Des Moines to a small stronghold they built in 1834 near the confluence of that river with the Mississippi. It lasted two years before being abandoned.

In the late spring of 1843, about sixty soldiers and civilians arrived on a steamboat at the confluence of the Raccoon and Des Moines Rivers just south of the present-day downtown capital city and began building another outpost. Located on point of land overlooking the rivers, this too was called Fort Des Moines and had about twenty-five buildings. Some were log structures built on limestone foundations. Others were made of brick. At one point, the fort's commander, Captain James Allen, recommended to his superiors that the station be named "Fort Raccoon" after the nearby river. They turned him down, and Fort Des Moines it became.

On an October night in 1845, a rifle shot followed by others near the fort announced the official opening of lands around the fort for settlement. In the following hours, settlers quickly claimed thousands of acres.

In May 1846, the fort was decommissioned and faded into obscurity, but the name stuck for the community that had grown around it. In 1855, government offices were moved from the original state capitol in Iowa City to the city of Fort Des Moines, and two years later, the word "fort" was dropped from the name.

Now, Des Moines is the largest city in Iowa with more than 218,000 residents, although more than 626,000 people live in the metro area.

Bauder's Ice Cream

If there's a place in Des Moines that people like to visit for cold treats, it's Bauder's Ice Cream, where frosty concoctions delight the eyes and taste buds. Opening as Bauder Pharmacy in 1916, it had the soda fountain in it from the start. For a while, people could watch the ice cream being hand-cranked in the front window, but health officials didn't like that, so making the ice cream, which is 12 percent butterfat, was moved to a back room. The ice cream comes in twenty-nine flavors ranging from the usuals like vanilla and chocolate to butter brickle and mocha chocolate. Flavors such as strawberry and peach appear seasonally when the fruits are ripe.

Visitors sit on twelve stools topped with blue cushions at a marble counter, or they can sit in a booth. The floor is multicolored hexagonal tiles, and overhead is a pressed tin ceiling. A Coca-Cola dispenser is on the counter, and tall, curved shiny spigots dispense carbonated water. Ice cream comes in shakes, malts, sundaes, floats and sodas or straight up in dishes and cones. Other than cones and to-go orders, everything is served on china plates or in sparkling glassware.

Bauder's is also known for its sandwiches, from peanut butter and jelly to tuna, chicken or ham salad and grilled cheese. The Reuben and the Roosevelt, which has turkey, swiss and mustard on rye, are the specialty sandwiches.

Every year since 1986, Bauder's sells ice cream at a booth at the Iowa State Fair in Des Moines. In 2001, Bauder's came up with a new treat that has proven to be a hit—the Peppermint Bar. With crushed Oreos for its top and bottom, its peppermint ice cream core is topped by fudge sauce. The two-and-a-half-inch cubes were sold only at the state fair for years, but now Bauder's sells them at its storefront year-round. Other bars have appeared including the Buddha Bar and the Coffee Latte Bar.

Fort Des Moines Museum

The third Fort Des Moines opened in 1901 as a 640-acre post for a cavalry unit. In 1917, the only officer candidate school for African Americans in the U.S. Army was established here. Its first graduation class in October of that year had 639 second lieutenants. Among them were 100 medical doctors and 12 dentists.

At the beginning of World War II, the army created another first at the post—a training center for the Women's Army Auxiliary Corps, later renamed the Women's Army Corps. More than 35,000 women applied for the first 1,000 positions that were open when training began in July 1942. About 125 were enlisted ranks, and 436 were officer candidates. Of the latter, 38 were black and, although they trained with white candidates, the two groups were later assigned to segregated units. Approximately 72,000 women trained here during the war but none for combat.

After the war, parts of the fort were sold off except for a barracks. That was converted into the Fort Des Moines Museum & Education Center, which opened in 2004 with interactive exhibits to tell the story of the officers and enlisted personnel who trained here during World War II.

Fort Des Moines was the training center for African American officers during World War I and for women officers, too, during World War II.

Iowa Capitol

The Iowa Capitol is unique in that where more than half of the other state capitols have one dome, this one has five. The largest, covered with gold leaf, topped by a cupola and rising to 278 feet above the ground, crowns the center of the tan-colored building. Four smaller domes wrapped in green copper and trimmed with gold-covered braid are atop the building's rectangular corners. Tall columns dominate the west and east façades, and large windows are on the major parts of the building. Iowa quarries supplied the stone and granite used in the building.

Tour guides provide information and tours of the building and its grounds, which have many statues and memorials. Also, on the first floor are offices of the executive branch and the former chambers of the Iowa Supreme Court which is now in another building. When the building opened in 1882, a circular floor of glass tile occupied the center of the first floor directly under the dome. That was removed in 1915, but in 2011 a replica of that floor was installed as part of a multiyear restoration of the capitol.

High above, a panel painted as a Civil War Medal of Honor is suspended just below the dome's interior, which is painted with a blue sky and white clouds.

Farther down from the dome are amber-colored metal sheets and tall clerestory windows. Half-circle paintings called lunettes represent the progress of humans, covering hunting, herding, agriculture, industry,

Completed in 1882, the Iowa Capitol is the third building to serve as the statehouse. It's also the only capitol in the nation with five domes.

commerce, education, science and the arts. Statues on pedestals between the lunettes depict history, science, law, fame, literature, industry, peace, commerce, agriculture, victory, truth and progress.

Tours of the capitol include going up in the eighty-foot-wide dome to an area called the Whispering Gallery, but mention should be given that this level is 130 steps up from the second floor. It is possible to go higher but only when sponsored by a legislator or an office holder.

The chambers of the House of Representatives and Senate are in the north and south wings of the second floor, respectively, and each has its unique décor including ceilings and skylights. The desks in the chambers are the originals although equipped now with electrical, communications and internet connections. The five-level law library occupies the west wing on the second floor, and many visitors remark that it is one of the more beautiful rooms with its wood and white wrought-iron railings lining the stacks and two circular staircases.

The capitol's grand staircase, made of marble, is in the east wing and connects the second and third floors.

The building is rich with ornate, colorful tile floors, murals and paintings by famous artists, mosaics, chandeliers, statues, twenty-nine types of marble from Iowa, Tennessee, Ohio and several nations, stained-glass windows and etched glass. Woods used in furniture, trim and carvings include red and white oak, black and white walnut, chestnut, cherry, mahogany and white and yellow pine.

People can visit the statehouse on their own or take free tours arranged at the tour guide desk on the ground floor. Cellphones can access information by calling 515-802-3004, and smartphones can retrieve audio and video signals at more than sixty stops in and around the capitol.

Iowa State Fair

While the Iowa State Fair may not be the oldest or largest state fair, it's possibly the most well-known—especially since it has served as the setting of a novel, a musical and movies all titled *State Fair*. Iowa's is ranked seventh among state fairs with 1.13 million visitors at last count.

The state fair started in Fairfield in 1854 and was there the following year. Over the next two decades, it was held in Muscatine, Oskaloosa, Iowa City, Dubuque, Burlington, Clinton, Keokuk and Cedar Rapids. In 1878, it moved to Des Moines because of its central location and, eight years later, was permanently relocated to what had been a farm on the city's east side.

By the time the first fair opened in the new location in Des Moines, sixty-seven buildings had been built on the grounds. Pioneer Hall, which was used for poultry exhibits, is now the oldest building at the fair and is part of the fair's museum complex with antiques and craftspeople showing visitors what they make the old-fashioned way. The museum area has Heritage Village, which consists of nineteenth-century buildings such as a farmhouse, post office, school, general store and barbershop.

Other brick-faced buildings from the early twentieth century still standing include the Livestock Pavilion, built in 1902 with fans that drew in fresh air and expelled the foul. Now, it's totally climate controlled. Opened in 1904, the Agriculture Building remains a fine example of the architecture style that appeared in many early twentieth-century expositions across the country. The Horse Barn, which has had four additions since it opened in 1907, has 398 horse stalls under its two-acre roof. The Administration Building, with its wide veranda, opened in 1908 and still holds the fair's administrative offices. In 1909, the racetrack opened, and modifications have expanded the grandstand to 14,500 seats. Machinery Hall, built in 1911, is now an exhibition structure called the Varied Industries Building. Many other buildings and facilities across the 450-acre fairgrounds have been restored in a massive program in the last several years.

The Agriculture Building holds one of the fair's more popular exhibits, the "Butter Cow." Each year since 1911, a sculptor works inside a glass-walled, forty-degree room fashioning a realistic, life-size cow out of about six hundred pounds of butter applied over a wire frame. Each butter cow is more than five feet tall and eight feet long and has enough butter to spread across nineteen thousand slices of toast. The first one was made by John Karl Daniels, a Norwegian immigrant, who typically made his sculptures of stone and metal but in 1900 accepted an offer to make a butter cow for the Minnesota State Fair. The first one he made at the Iowa fair depicted a young boy leading a calf to its mother. Since then, he and succeeding sculptors have created butter cows that have been accompanied by varying companions over the years—astronaut Neil Armstrong, a Waterloo John Boy Tractor, the cartoon characters of *Peanuts*, Elvis, Harry Potter, a Harley-Davidson motorcycle, Snow White and the Seven Dwarves and a rendition of *The Field of Dreams*.

Already popular with Iowans, the fair became more widely known through Iowan Phil Stong's 1932 novel *State Fair*, which uses it as the main setting. In it, a farm couple travels to the fair with their teenage son and daughter. While the father's hog wins a blue ribbon—as do the mother's pickles—the fair, with its bright lights, appeals seductively to the son and daughter. He falls for a carnival girl, but she tells him she doesn't want the comparatively dull life on a farm. The daughter is attracted to another worldly traveler, a newspaper reporter, yet after a tryst in a grove of trees, she realizes she would not like traveling to big cities like he wants to do. In the end, the family, with the teens sad but wise, returns to the safe life of a farm.

The book became a best-seller even though some readers frowned on the moral temptations facing the son and daughter. Even Stong's hometown library banned it. Yet it became a 1933 movie nominated for two Academy Awards, including Best Picture. *State Fair* was made into two more big-screen movies, a TV movie and a musical that played on Broadway.

The eleven-day state fair always ends on the Sunday that falls two weeks before Labor Day.

Jordan House

When Virginian James Jordan moved to the Des Moines area in 1846, he first lived in a tent and then a log cabin. Construction on this house began in 1850 and continued over a few years. Jordan, who raised and sold cattle, served as a state senator and representative plus was on the county board of supervisors and helped establish the State Bank of Des Moines.

In the years before the Civil War, Jordan used his property as a major stop on the Underground Railroad, a series of safe places runaway slaves could use when traveling to freedom farther north. Here, they rested in outbuildings, fields and barns. The abolitionist John Brown was here at least twice, once in 1858 when leading up to two dozen slaves out of bondage.

The two-story, white-painted house was also a popular meeting place for politicians and business leaders and a welcome rest stop for those traveling to and from the west.

Because several railroads met in this area, the Chicago Rock Island and Pacific Railroad built maintenance shops, a roundhouse and switching yards here, unofficially known as Valley Junction. That became the official name of the city in 1873 until the city was renamed as West Des Moines.

The West Des Moines Historical Society administers the Jordan House.

Living History Farms

Living History Farms opened in 1970 in Urbandale (part of the metro Des Moines area) as an open-air museum and covers five hundred acres. Truly, with one exception, nothing historic occurred here, but it represents what happened in different places and times in Iowa with three farms and a town composed of authentic buildings gathered from across the state. Interpreters at the sites explain what's going on in those areas.

The 1700 Ioway Farm represents how the Ioway (pronounced I-O-Way) lived during the initial stages of contact with European American cultures. In the summer, *náhachi*—lodges made of bark—provided cool retreats from the heat. When winter settled in, the Ioway built *chákirutha*, huts fashioned out of cattail leaves, to keep them warm. Also, when traveling on long hunts for buffalo and other game, the Ioway used hides to erect *chibóthraje*, or tipis, as temporary shelters made of buffalo hides and poles that could easily be put up, taken down and pulled by people or animals. They also planted gardens, usually with corn, squash and beans, constructed racks to dry food

Above: One of the farms at the Living History Farms depicts that of the Ioway, one of the earlier indigenous people living in the state.

Opposite: A site interpreter works at the stove in the 1900 Farm's house at Living History Farms.

and scrape hides, built sweat lodges and more. Until they began trading with the first elements of European Americans for items made of metal, Ioway tools were made of bone and stone.

When settlers began arriving in Iowa in the middle of the nineteenth century, their life was about as harsh as it was for the Ioway, as is demonstrated at the 1850s Pioneer Farm. They built log cabins, hoping to build better quarters such as frame houses in the future. Their barns were more like storage sheds than animal shelters. Fences were made of wood split into rails. Smokehouses preserved meats. Corn was raised to feed cattle and hogs, which were then sold for cash. The same went for chickens and eggs. Families ate what they raised in gardens.

Oxen pulled carts and plows to open the grasslands. It was hard work considering that the roots of some prairie grasses could go down twenty feet and had woven together over thousands of years.

The Industrial Revolution led to the creation of machinery that could help farmers. At the 1900 Horse-Drawn Farm, large draft horses made a farm successful by pulling plows, planters, harvesting equipment and wagons. Corn was still the main crop, now followed by hay and oats.

Larger barns were built. The use of hot water permitted foods to be preserved in bottles and crockery. Some machines and steam-powered tractors appeared, as did improvements to the quality of life in the form of cast-iron stoves and telephones.

Although the small community of Walnut Hill represents a fictional town of the 1870s, its buildings are real. Each was used in its original purpose elsewhere in Iowa. These include a drugstore, a bank, a newspaper office, a millinery, a law office, a vet clinic, a general store—where visitors can purchase some goods—a family home and working blacksmith, pottery and broom-making shops.

Besides the regular visits, special dinners for up to twelve guests featuring foods from the late nineteenth century are held during winter months at the 1900 farmhouse, the family home in Walnut Hill and the Victorian mansion, where teas are also served in December and April.

The one building marking a historic event is the Church of the Land in Walnut Hill. It was built where Saint Pope John Paul II held an outdoor Mass in front of 350,000 people on October 4, 1979. It remains the largest gathering of people in Iowa. The nondenominational church was built to look like one that would be found in the time frame of Walnut Hill.

Terrace Hill

Built as the home of prominent Des Moines businessman Benjamin Franklin Allen, Iowa's first millionaire, this three-story brick Italianate mansion with a square tower now serves as the official home for the Iowa governor and is called Terrace Hill.

Finished in 1869 at a cost of $400,000 for it and thirty acres of land, the mansion had gas lights, hot and cold water, indoor restrooms and an elevator. The grounds featured walkways, formal gardens, a fountain, a greenhouse and an arbor.

Built as a businessman's home in 1869, Terrace Hill is now the official residence of the Iowa governor.

Financial problems forced Allen to declare bankruptcy in 1875. In 1883, he sold the eighteen-thousand-square-foot mansion and eight acres for $60,000 to Frederick M. Hubbell, who was involved with railroads, insurance companies and real estate. Hubbell's descendants lived in the mansion until 1957. Then it sat empty until 1971, when they donated it to the state to serve as the governor's residence.

The fourteen-foot-high doors at first-floor entry are solid walnut and weigh four hundred pounds each. Rooms on the first floor, which are sometimes used for official purposes, include the reception room, a formal dining room, a drawing room, music rooms, a sitting room and the library, all connected by the wide main hall. The grand staircase at the end of the hall features polished rosewood bannisters and leads to the second floor. Halfway to the second floor is a landing colorfully lit by a nine-by-thirteen-foot stained-glass window installed in the 1880s.

Of the four bedrooms that were on the second floor, two are still there for guests of the first family. The other two are now offices for the governor and the governor's spouse. The governor's working office is at the capitol.

The rooms are furnished with Victorian-era furniture, some of which was owned by the Hubbells. Parquet floors can be seen in areas that are not carpeted. Walls and ceilings are painted with decorative details. Heavy pocket doors separate some rooms, and a seven-and-a-half-foot-tall chandelier with two thousand crystals hangs in the drawing room. One fireplace is made of pink Spanish marble. Paintings, including one by Grant Wood, hang on the walls.

Terrace Hill is one of the more accessible governors' mansions in the nation, and architectural historians regard it as one of the best examples of Second Empire architecture.

Hour-long guided tours begin in the carriage house on the west side of Terrace Hill. No tours are given of the mansion's third floor, as it is the private residence of the governor's family, nor are self-guided tours allowed.

GRINNELL

Merchants National Bank

Toward the end of architect Louis Sullivan's career, when large commissions were no longer coming his way, he accepted a request in 1906 to design a small bank in Owatonna, Minnesota. The bank's owner said he did not want a bank designed in the prominent architectural style of the day—a Greek temple with columns—and Sullivan delivered. His design was a brick building shaped like a cube and rich with terra-cotta details and arched windows bearing stained-glass windows.

Soon, offers to design similar buildings came to Sullivan and he created seven more, six of them banks along with one office building. Resembling ornate strong boxes that held valuables, this group of buildings became known as Sullivan's "Jewel Boxes."

On a downtown corner in Grinnell, Merchants National Bank was Sullivan's fourth jewel box, and it opened on New Year's Day 1915. Above the entry, a large, buff-colored terra-cotta portal, filled with ornamental designs and geometric shapes

The elaborate ornamental entry on the Merchant's National Bank shows the detail that architect Louis Sullivan put into his designs.

plus a rose window made of blue, green and yellow stained-glass, dominates the building's otherwise austere south façade made of red-brown brick. Two winged golden lions guard the front doors. On the east wall are a fifteen-by-forty-foot stained-glass window and gold columns.

The side window, the rose window and a skylight flood the two-story open interior of the bank with colored light. Additional light is supplied by Sullivan-designed fixtures that hang about halfway down from the two-story-high ceiling. More lighting comes from desk lamps on a simple but striking check-writing table in the center of the marble floor. That table, the floor and other items such as the clock surrounded by a colorful mosaic above the entrance remain as designed by Sullivan.

When the director of one bank asked Sullivan why he should be paid more than other architects competing to design a building, Sullivan replied, "A thousand architects could design those buildings. Only I can design this one."

Merchants National Bank is now occupied by the Grinnell Chamber of Commerce, which welcome visitors during business hours on weekdays and by appointment otherwise.

HAVERHILL

Matthew Edel Blacksmith Shop

Blacksmiths have been around since people learned to control fire thousands of years ago and were numerous until the middle of the nineteenth century. That's when factories of the Industrial Revolution began churning out metal items faster and cheaper than blacksmiths could make them. They were the people who used iron, steel and heat to create metal objects that were practical or decorative or both. In most small towns that dotted Iowa more than one hundred years ago, one could find a blacksmith. They made hammers, hoes, shovels, nails, rims for wooden wagon wheels, horseshoes, hinges, knives and drawer handles. If someone needed something that was metal, a blacksmith could usually make it.

Matthew Edel emigrated from Stuttgart, Germany, and eventually made his way to the small town of Haverhill, which is about seven miles southwest of Marshalltown. Here, he opened his blacksmith shop in 1883, when he was twenty-seven years old. Shortly after he and Maria Hoffman married, they lived on the shop's second floor. In 1890, he built the Victorian home next to the shop, and the couple raised eight children there. A summer kitchen is also on the property

Like many blacksmiths, Edel was an inventor too and patented his creations. Scraps of iron wheel rims became dehorning clippers used to remove the horns of cattle. Another invention stretched wire to repair fences. He created tools for people making or repairing carriages and wagons. Edel also made iron crosses that some people preferred to stone markers in cemeteries.

Besides making items for local customers, Edel advertised his creations and ran a mail-order business. He sold hoes for $1.35 each although he charged less when they were ordered in bulk.

The shop, now a state historic site and not a reconstruction, is dark inside, as if the soot that settled on everything over the years sucks up whatever light gets in there. The place looks like Edel just stepped out the door and will return in a moment. Like many blacksmiths, he made many of the tools he used, including radial arm and band saws. He modernized in 1915 and started working on cars.

Everything in Edel's shop centers on the brick forge, where coal was burned to heat the metals that Edel bent, stretched and hammered into the

German immigrant Matthew Edel Smith was twenty-seven when he opened his blacksmith shop in the small town of Haverhill in 1883.

shapes he wanted. When gas engines became available, he connected one to turn a line shaft that ran across the shop ceiling. Spinning belts and pulleys, the line shaft powered saws, a drill press, a trip hammer and other tools. Early on, Edel pumped the big bellows that fed air into the forge to get the most heat possible out of the coal. Later, he attached the bellows to the line shaft. Finally, he used an electric fan to blow air on the forge.

After Edel died in 1940, one of his seven sons, Louis, who had been helping his father for some years, took over the business but left the blacksmith shop alone, choosing to work in the addition that housed their auto repair business. Louis died in May 1978, and the family donated the shop to the State Historical Society of Iowa in 1986.

The Matthew Edel Blacksmith Shop is open from Memorial Day to Labor Day.

JEFFERSON

RVP ~ 1875

When visitors step into RVP ~ 1875 in downtown Jefferson, they may think they're looking at historical furniture. Nope. The furniture they see has been made to look antique by owner Robby Pedersen, who uses tools made before

1875. Among his tools are more than five hundred wood body planes, about half of which were made before the Civil War, an 1860 foot-powered lathe and a hand-powered rip saw from 1870. Unable to find an authentic shaving horse from the nineteenth century, Pedersen built one to sit on while shaping dowels, handles and pegs.

Located in—fittingly—a former lumberyard, the woodshop shows about one hundred pieces of Pedersen's creations including wardrobes, a slat-back bed, stools, cupboards, sideboards, benches and writing desks for homes. Pedersen also fashions 1875-era furniture for offices. He makes about seventy pieces of 1870s-era furniture annually, about the same number of pieces a wood craftsman would produce in the late nineteenth century.

Even though RVP ~ 1875 is open 9:00 a.m. to 5:00 p.m. Monday through Friday, Pedersen prefers visitors make appointments.

LYNNVILLE

Wagaman Mill

When John Sparks moved from eastern Iowa to Lynnville in 1845, he set out to harness the power of the North Skunk River, which flows by the town. He built a small watermill the following year but, apparently seeing greater potential, erected a larger one in 1848 that still stands. Sparks also built a wooden dam behind which pent-up waters could be channeled to turn the big paddlewheel of his mill to grind grains. Sparks's business took off, supported by farmers from miles around who wanted their wheat ground.

Sparks sold the mill in 1851, and that began a succession of owners and users. In 1868, Nathan and Joseph Arnold diverted the water from turning the external wooden wheel to flowing around a metal water wheel that spun a vertical shaft. That was more efficient than the paddlewheel. Thirty years later, W.K. Wagaman bought the mill and modernized it more, something his son Fred continued to do. Fred also built a concrete dam in 1918 to replace the wooden one, which had been washed away in a flood. As grinding wheat became unprofitable, Fred turned to milling corn and animal feed in 1925. That same year, he installed a 2,300-volt generator and began producing electricity for area residents. The mill has also been used over the years to saw lumber and aid in the production of cloth. In 1958, the equipment in the mill was completely electrified.

Built in 1848, the Wagaman Mill in Lynville was used to grind wheat, corn meal and animal feed, saw wood, generate electricity and help in the production of cloth.

Restoration efforts began in 1973 to return some areas of the mill to their original condition. This included the vertical turbine the Arnold brothers installed in 1868. In 1977, James Leffel & Company in Ohio reported that the turbine is the oldest of its products operating in the world. The Lynnville Historical Society operates the historical site.

PRAIRIE CITY

Neal Smith National Wildlife Refuge

Settlers arriving in Iowa in the middle of the nineteenth century saw an endless tall-grass prairie that covered more than 80 percent of the young state's land. Now, less than .1 percent of Iowa's native tall-grass prairie remains, and what does remain is scattered across the state, mostly in small patches. The largest parcel of prairie is 3,000 acres north of Sioux City. The next-largest tract is only 240 acres in northeast Iowa.

Neal Smith National Wildlife Refuge was created in 1990 by the U.S. Fish and Wildlife Service to restore the tall-grass prairie and oak savanna that were the main ecosystems for thousands of years here before they were nearly eradicated, starting in the nineteenth century, for agricultural purposes. Of the refuge's authorized 8,645 acres, only 90 are original prairie. Restoring a prairie is difficult. Even by sowing the ground with seeds gathered from plants growing in remnants, the best a restored prairie can support is about one hundred species, far fewer than the four hundred types of plants that can be found in a piece of native prairie.

Fire is one way to manage the prairie, which is something Native Americans did for centuries. While it may be thought that lightning caused the fires that swept the prairies, researchers state that Indians deliberately set the majority of them. To the Indians, a prairie fire was called the Red Buffalo.

Large fires drove game such as bison, elk and deer toward other Indians waiting to kill them. Another way indigenous people used fire was to burn old grasses, causing new tender and tasty shoots to grow. That enticed the bison and other animals to those areas, which made hunting them predictable. Fires were used to even protect some plants such as those with medicinal values. By carefully burning away other plants around the ones they wanted to save, Indians created areas where nothing was left to burn—in essence, fireproof zones.

Fires set at various times of year promoted the growth of different plants. For example, fires set in the fall cause more flowers to bloom the next spring. Indians also used fire in celebrations, to literally smoke out enemies, signal one another and obscure hunters' movements.

Young trees and woody plants trying to invade the prairie were killed by the fires and didn't have much chance to overtake the prairie.

A bison and her calf cause a prairie-style traffic jam at Neal Smith National Wildlife Refuge.

However, most European Americans viewed fire as an enemy and prevented it whenever possible. By building farm fields, roads and communities, the new arrivals on the prairie created firebreaks that stymied the prairie fires. Soon, invasive plants and woods began to overtake the original landscape.

Utilizing what worked for thousands of years to rejuvenate the prairie and hold trees and woody plants at bay, the staff at Neal Smith NWR occasionally sets fire to parts of the prairie on the refuge.

Miles of paved trails for hikers and bicyclists lead from the visitor center, which has fine displays about the natural history and the qualities of the prairie and oak tree savanna that make up the land here.

For many visitors, the refuge's main attraction is the one-and-a-half-mile road that leads through an area where about fifty buffalo and twenty elk roam freely. No one is allowed out of the vehicles, and the animals always have the right of way, which can cause some interesting traffic stoppages. Also, because the animals can wander about their eight-hundred-acre enclosure, they may not always be in sight of those traveling on the road.

SCRANTON

Lincoln Highway Markers

One of two rare concrete markers with busts of President Abraham Lincoln are alongside the route of the Lincoln Highway, the first auto route across the nation.

North of Scranton, James E. Moss erected two rare markers to honor Abraham Lincoln in 1926 and mark the route of the Lincoln Highway, which passed alongside his farmland. A veteran who lost a foot in the Civil War, Moss commissioned Harold Carlisle of Jefferson to create the large concrete markers. On its front, each has an L for the Lincoln Highway and "J.E. Moss" since the farmer was also using these as boundary markers. Atop each was a bust of Lincoln; the originals were lost but have been replaced.

One is a mile north of the intersection of State Highway 25 and U.S. 30 and is on the west side of the road. The other is two hundred yards away as the road curves to the west on County Road E29. It's on the south side of that road.

STORY CITY

Story City Antique Carousel

Elaborately carved horses are among the wonderful creations at the Story City Carousel, which was made in 1913.

A group of horses is called a herd. Similarly, a number of dogs is a pack, and a bunch of chickens is a flock. But what does one call a group of horses, dogs and chickens? A carousel!

For being an item that has brought amusement to untold numbers of people, the origins of carousels go back more than one thousand years when they were used to train men for war. Knights returning from the Crusades in the Middle East brought back a game, or an exercise, where men carrying lances would ride their horses in a circle and try to snare a metal ring hanging from a post with their lances. The Spanish called it *carosella*, meaning "little war."

For a long time, learning to spear was the sole purpose of a carousel. In the late 1700s in Europe, small, lightweight carousels featuring carved animals suspended from a center pole appeared as amusement rides. They were powered by animals and humans.

The advent of steam allowed the carousels to grow to about the size they are today, forty to fifty feet across. Ultimately, they were powered by electricity. The first ones in North America appeared in the 1860s. Many were built in parks. Portable ones traveled with circuses and carnivals. Riders sat on hand-carved extravaganzas—parade ponies, racing horses, horses of the imagination and a host of other creatures, including lions, ostriches, tigers and strutting chickens. Other items such as rotating tubs went around and around although chariots remained stationary. Jewels shone everywhere. Glass eyes beamed on the animals' faces. Some even had real horsehair. The animals moved up and down in a circle of bright colors, flashing mirrors and brilliant lights. Calliopes provided carnival music.

Carousels in the United States numbered as many as four thousand until they began to fall out of favor during the Depression. Some were demolished, and others were bought by antique collectors. Original carousel horses sell now from hundreds of dollars to beyond $20,000. Rides that aren't horses fetch more. A cat was listed for $22,000 in the last few years. A lion went for $23,000.

The Herschell-Spillman Company of Tonawanda, New York, the world's largest manufacturer of amusement rides, built a carousel in 1913 for P.T. Gifford in Grundy Center, Iowa. He took the carousel—designed to be portable—to town celebrations, county fairs and Fourth of July events in Iowa.

Story City acquired the carousel in 1938 for $1,200, which was paid off on the first weekend it was open. Later, a weather-proof shelter was built around it.

Everything on this carousel is hard-carved from poplar—twenty horses, two dogs, two chickens, two pigs, a couple of chariots and a tub that spins. All are set in double rows around the platform. A 1936 Wurlitzer calliope organ hidden in the center column provides the lively tunes.

TAMA

The Lincoln Highway and King Tower Cafe

In 1900, Iowa had 104,000 miles of roads. Traveling by car was almost limited to within the cities because they had roads good enough for vehicles to use. Most other roads in Iowa were dirt and poorly maintained. Driving on them when rain and snow turned them into mud was nearly impossible.

So, people rode trains when traveling between towns.

Wanting to tie the nation together with roads designed for motor vehicles, Carl F. Fisher, whose Indiana company made auto headlights, began a movement in 1912 to create a gravel coast-to-coast highway, to be called the Lincoln Highway, across thirteen states. In 1913, the first section was completed. It was less than four miles long and linked New York and New Jersey.

Ultimately it would cover 3,216 miles, with 358 of those miles being between Clinton and Council Bluffs, Iowa. In 1926, the United States started a numbered highway system, and the highway was renamed as

The only bridge on the entire Lincoln Highway to have the highway's name spelled out on its balustrade is in Tama.

U.S. Highway 30. However, people have continually called it the Lincoln Highway. In 1928, Boy Scouts erected 2,436 concrete guideposts marking the route in Iowa. By 1931, the entire highway within Iowa was paved.

A unique part of the Lincoln Highway stands on Tama's east side—a short concrete bridge. What sets it apart from other bridges are its balustrades, which spell out "Lincoln Highway." It's one of the few remaining structures associated with the original highway in the nation and is known to be the only bridge of this design. Unable to bear the rigors presented by modern traffic, it was moved from its original location and put on the east side of Tama, less than one hundred yards off Business U.S. 30 on East Fifth Street.

Still on U.S. 30 and a quarter mile east of the bridge is the King Tower Café. Built in 1937, the café was part of a one-stop complex that had an eighteen-cabin motel, wrecker service, a gas station and a garage, all of which are gone now—only the café remains. In the National Register of Historic Places, King Tower is known for serving good breakfasts, lunches and dinners in a quiet atmosphere.

Anyone interested in driving the original route of the Lincoln Highway in Iowa will find it at https://www.lincolnhighwayassoc.org/map/?state=iowa.

Meskwaki Settlement

The Meskwaki Settlement is about four miles west of the town of Toledo on U.S. 30. Some people mistakenly call it a reservation, but it is not federal land set aside for Native Americans. It is land owned by the Meskwaki (also spelled Mesquaki). For almost two centuries, they had been pushed south and west of their homelands near the Great Lakes, first by the French and their Native American allies and later by the United States to where they ultimately went to a Kansas reservation. Even though they had been moved there by the government, some Meskwaki initiated an effort to buy some of the land they had lived on in Iowa and were joined by about three hundred more who had somehow remained in Iowa while the others had moved to the west. In 1857, the Iowa legislature agreed to let the Meskwaki buy eighty acres for $1,000 from settlers who had taken over the land at the price of $0.10 an acre not that many years earlier.

The Meskwaki have bought more land over the years and now own more than 8,100 acres. They have built K–12 schools, a casino, a health clinic, a 404-room hotel, courts and departments of natural resources and public works. They also have their own police force. Approximately 1,400 people are enrolled in the Meskwaki Nation. Each August, the Meskwaki hold a four-day powwow that is open to the public.

6

SOUTH-CENTRAL IOWA

ALLERTON

International Center for Rural Culture and Art Inc.

In a state where most barns have boxy floor plans, and some have arched roofs resembling large lunch pails, round barns are rare. They evolved out of a movement that began building octagonal barns in the 1850s in the east and made their way to Iowa. As construction techniques improved, people began erecting round barns in the 1890s, and their popularity lasted until the 1930s. They were mostly made of wood but also stone, brick and hollow clay tile.

Some owners of circular barns claimed they were more efficient than the conventional rectangular barns. Also, because the structures' design gave them more strength, some people believed round barns could tolerate windstorms better the standard barns.

A nonprofit in Allerton, the International Center for Rural Culture and Art Inc., has a round barn, the Nelson Barn, at the heart of its collection of restored buildings associated with Iowa's past. Locals also call it the Fennell Barn to honor its builder, Ed Fennell. His wooden barn, which measures sixty feet across, was built in 1912 as a dairy barn. With no center support, its cavernous room covered eight milking stanchions, stalls for mules, a stall to hold a bull or a cow and its calf and some small grain bins. A pulley in the center of the ceiling once hauled hay to the loft.

The list is incomplete, but about 100 of the 140 round barns built in Iowa remain standing in various conditions. Of the 40 or so octagonal barns built, 13 remain.

Near the Fennell Barn is the Williams School, an 1869 one-room schoolhouse. Also here is a church with a name that might cause confusion, the New York Christian Church. Named after the state, the unincorporated community of New York, Iowa, also had a post office from 1856 to 1903. The church was used until the 1970s, and the center acquired it in 1998. A Victorian house built in 1897 for a Civil War veteran is the center's latest acquisition and is fully restored.

The center's buildings are open 1:00 p.m. to 5:00 p.m. Friday, Saturday and Sunday in the summer months or by appointment.

More about Barns

Anyone who has traveled across Iowa, especially off the interstate highways, has seen a preponderance of barns. Usually built of wood with some featuring brick and stone, they come in all sizes, shapes, configurations and colors, usually red followed by white. Older, unused barns are often weathered grays. To learn about barns, visit the Iowa Barn Foundation at www.iowabarnfoundation.org and note the "Barn Tours" link, which shows rotating seasonal tours of barns in different areas of the state.

Also, since about 2005, colorful "barn quilts" featuring wonderful designs have been appearing on many Iowa barns, following a movement that began in Ohio a few years earlier and has spread across the states.

BLAKESBURG

Antique Airfield, Airpower Museum and Antique Aviation Association

Sometimes on a warm day, a whisper of air barely nudges the clipped blades of grass that form the surface of the runway at Antique Airfield before rotating the orange windsock a quarter-turn atop a hangar. Beyond that, there's hardly a sound where two lines of low, gray metal buildings stand near a curve in County Road H41 a few miles east of Blakesburg. This is how most airports in the nation appeared in the 1930s.

The main building here is the Airpower Museum, where no ropes bar visitors from the aircraft. Many were made before World War II; some were built by their pilots. Of the museum's forty or so aircraft, fifteen to twenty are usually on display. Some are angular, boxy things with doped linen stretched across their wooden frames, and others are sleek with swooping, polished metal curves. Their richly painted surfaces almost glow in pools of light filtering through the skylights.

For those who like antique and unique aircraft, this patch of Iowa is another part of heaven. Among the aircraft are an American Eagle Eaglet B-31, a 1935 plane similar to what bush pilots used in the early day of flying in Alaska; one of three Pietenpol Sky Scouts built in 1933; and a 1943 Aeronca 65-TC is what was called an L-3 observation plane by the army in World War II. A Republic RC3 Seabee built in the 1940s can put down on land or water. A two-seat Ryan PT-22 trained fledgling pilots in the United States and other countries during World War II. The Stinson JR(S), built in 1931, may have hauled components of an atomic bomb. A Welch OW-8, which looks like a flying insect, is the only one known to be in a museum.

Antique and homebuilt aircraft are displayed in the hangars at the Antique Airfield, Airpower Museum and Antique Aviation Association just east of Blakesburg.

One area in the buildings is dedicated to the Sixth Air Force, a virtually unknown U.S. air command of World War II charged with protecting the Panama Canal. Another room has aircraft engines, models hanging from the ceiling, posters on the walls and many other aviation-related artifacts. An airplane is usually being worked on in the restoration center. If the doors are open on one of the two main hangars, visitors might find someone who will take time from working on an airplane to talk awhile.

The Antique Aviation Association holds a convention here for about five days every August. Open only to AAA members, the fly-in attracts 350 to 400 homebuilts, classics and antiques along with around 1,700 people. Most of the aviators come to visit one another, watch planes rumble between the runway and the display area and swap stories, real and exaggerated, in the Pilot's Pub. If a person who doesn't belong to AAA wants to attend, joining the association can be done at any time, including during the convention.

ELDON

American Gothic House

A building usually becomes famous for one of two reasons—something important happened there or its architecture is unique, by design or construction. However, the residence built by Charles Dibble in the small town of Eldon in the early 1880s became famous because of how it was painted—but not by a house painter. Iowa artist Grant Wood used it in the background of his most famous painting, *American Gothic*, which depicts what many people thought—and still believe—to be a farmer and his wife in front of their farmhouse.

Wood began learning art in high school in Cedar Rapids and studied styles of art in Minneapolis and the Art Institute of Chicago. He also journeyed to Europe four times to study a variety of styles, including impressionism and post-impressionism. Wood accepted commissions for different types of art, including painting the walls of a sleeping porch of a Cedar Rapids mansion. He also designed a twenty-by-twenty-four-foot stained-glass window for the Veterans Memorial in Cedar Rapids. While overseeing the manufacturing of the stained-glass pieces in Germany, he became acquainted with the paintings of the Northern Renaissance style, including those of Hans Memling.

Upon returning to the states, Wood began to use what he had learned in Germany in his paintings. His *Woman and Plants* and *Stone City* were the first indications of his change in style.

In August 1930, Wood visited Eldon, about a 105-mile drive south of his Cedar Rapids studio-home, where eighteen-year-old artist John Sharp drove him around town. As they went up a hill east of downtown, Wood saw a house and asked Sharp to stop the car. Intrigued with the Gothic-shaped window at the front of the house's second floor, Wood sketched the house on the back of an envelope. To him, the window was pretentious, belonging in a church more than a simple midwestern house with white-painted board-and-batten walls. "Cardboardy," Wood called the house.

Actually, the window—and its twin at the rear of the upper story—had a purpose. The original owner, Dibble, bought them because they could be opened so wide that large furniture could be hauled in and out of the second-floor bedrooms without having to negotiate the narrow interior stairs.

The day after he saw the house, Wood returned to create a quick oil painting of it after receiving permission from its owners, Gideon and Mary Hart Jones. He thought the house might be right for a painting he had in mind to enter in the upcoming forty-ninth annual competitive exhibit put on by the Art Institute of Chicago.

Wood then went to his Cedar Rapids studio to work on the thirty-by-twenty-five-inch painting in which he initially envisioned a woman standing next to a man holding a rake in front of their house. In his mind, they were a father and his spinster daughter. Wood's sister Nan Wood Graham had posed for him in several earlier paintings, and she agreed to sit (or actually stand) for this one, too. Despite modeling as the unmarried daughter, Graham had been married a few years by then. However, she lived with her brother and their mother in his studio-home because her husband had tuberculosis and was confined to a hospital.

Wood envisioned the man as a widower. He asked his Cedar Rapids dentist, Dr. Byron McKeeby, to pose, but McKeeby was reluctant. He was afraid people would recognize him, and he did not want the notoriety of appearing in a painting. When Wood said he would not make McKeeby recognizable, the dentist relented.

First, Wood painted the house in his studio. A chimney that existed in a sketch did not make it to the final painting, which took weeks to complete. At one point, Wood had another Gothic window in view on the house's single-story addition. That, too, went away. Wood steepened the roof's slope and elongated the window.

For her part, Wood told his sister to slick her hair back and sew rickrack around the neckline of a print coverall apron he had ordered through the mail—she said years later that she had actually selected the apron from a store. Since rickrack was out of style as a trim, Graham ripped some from her mother's dresses to sew on the apron. The brooch she wears in the painting belonged to their mother and features Persephone, goddess of vegetation and the underworld.

As she had done before, Graham posed in the mornings in the natural light falling into her brother's studio from the belfry atop the building. Wood then gathered his canvas and materials to visit McKeeby at his office in the evenings to work him into the painting. The artist had McKeeby wear coveralls and hold a theatrical prop pitchfork.

Wood arranged Graham and McKeeby in the style of many nineteenth-century photos made of midwestern families standing in front of their sod houses, bodies erect and eyes usually dead ahead. When Wood told his sister how he was going to paint the figures with long faces, she protested that her face was too round. He agreed, saying, "Your face is too round, but I can stretch it out long."

So he did, elongating her face just as he did with the house's features. However, Wood didn't have to alter the sixty-two-year-old McKeeby's naturally long face. He then further emphasized the scene's verticality with the pitchfork's long tines, which are replicated in the seams of the father's coveralls, the vertical panels of the house's board-and-batten walls, the lines of the man's open coat and his shirt stripes.

When finished, Wood neatly signed his name over the lower right panel of the coveralls and shipped the painting plus his *Stone City* painting (also completed in 1930—it won the best landscape award at the Iowa State Fair that summer) to Chicago.

Initially, the exhibition's jury rejected *American Gothic*. However, a former trustee of the institute saw that it had not been accepted and approached the chair of the jury to say an obvious mistake had been made in ignoring it. Eventually, *American Gothic* was chosen for the show, which ran from October 1 to December 14, 1930.

The first that Wood knew his painting was not only accepted for the show but also had been awarded third place was when he read about it in the local newspaper over breakfast. At first, he and Graham thought the newspaper had made a mistake. Only when a reporter soon asked Wood to comment on *American Gothic* did they realize the story was true. While he was pleased with the honor, he was concerned because the institute had

A couple strikes a familiar pose in front of the house in Eldon that was used by artist Grant Wood in the background of his painting *American Gothic*.

a string attached to it—a $300 purchase prize. Wood was uncomfortable about letting the picture go, but since times were tough in the Depression, he accepted the money. He then hired a publicist to inform newspapers in several cities about *American Gothic*.

Although works by Guy Pène du Bois and Louis Ritman won the higher awards and more money, everyone talked about *American Gothic*. Remarks about it came from everywhere, including that it depicted reality, it was a parody of the American farmer, the woman was his daughter, the woman was his wife, she looks at him as if he's about to die, it's insulting to Iowans, it's an insult to Americans, what does the name *American Gothic* mean, the woman's face would sour milk, why is a man his age marrying a woman so much younger than he is, what's with that tendril of hair hanging behind her ear and someone must be dead because why else would the house's curtains be down in the daytime.

Wood commented occasionally about the painting. At one time, he wrote, "The people in 'American Gothic' are not farmers but are small-town, as the shirt on the man indicates. They are American, however, and it is unfair to localize them to Iowa," and "The painting has been spoken of sometimes as satire, but I didn't mean it so. I admire the people in that painting."

For Wood, the painting's reception catapulted him into the major leagues and established him as a major member of the American Regionalism movement in art. As McKeeby had feared, people said he was the man in the painting, something he denied for five years before admitting that he had posed for Wood.

Although the house gained fame because of the painting and became known as the "American Gothic House," it remained a private residence for years. It even sat empty during some of the 1970s. Weather and vandalism were concerns to people hoping to preserve it. In 1991, the State Historical Society of Iowa acquired the house and renovated it a year later.

A visitor center opened in 2007 with exhibits relating to Wood, the painting and the house. It also has several print aprons with white rickrack necklines and black coats for visitors to wear as they pose in front of the house just a few yards away.

Grant Wood died in 1942, when he was fifty, and is buried in Anamosa's Riverside Cemetery where a sleeping lion lies across his tombstone. Nan Wood Graham died in 1990 at the age of ninety-one. Dr. Byron McKeeby died in 1950 when he was eighty-three.

Unless it is on loan to other art museums, *American Gothic* hangs in the American Art section, Gallery 263, at the Art Institute of Chicago.

MAHASKA AND MONROE COUNTIES

Muchakinock and Buxton

Two of the most racially integrated communities in the United States existed in south-central Iowa more than a century ago. Muchakinock and Buxton were mining communities where miners of equal rank were paid the same salary, everyone paid the same rent for good housing, their children went to the same schools, injury and death benefits were identical among the races and many social functions were open to all. White merchants had stores next to black shopkeepers. Black and white doctors and the hospitals provided medical care for both races, and one doctor, Edward A. Carter, was the first black man to graduate from the University of Iowa College of Medicine.

The two towns came about for two reasons: coal and the Consolidation Coal Company.

Coal had developed under Iowa's rich topsoil for millions of years, spread across a third of the state in formations that stretched across the southernmost counties and rose like a pyramid that topped out in north-central Iowa. While some coal was found in exposed seams in hillsides and bluffs that had collapsed, most was underground.

Some Native Americans may have used what they found, much like the Hopi in Arizona did as early as AD 1300. Settlers arriving in Iowa used coal they found for heating their homes and cooking. Lem Brattain opened the first commercial coal mine near Farmington in southeast Iowa in 1840. He sold some locally, hauled more to Keokuk twenty-five miles away and sold supplies to riverboats traveling on the Des Moines River. Slowly, more mines opened in Iowa, but none were big. Some sold coal to nearby blacksmiths. In 1850, only 1,500 tons of coal were produced in the state.

Then the railroads began expending miles of tracks across the continent. In 1850, 9,051 miles laced the United States together. A decade later, the country had 30,626 miles of tracks; in 1870, 52,922 miles; and in 1880, 93,267 miles. With this expansion came an increased appetite for coal to power the steam locomotives.

Iowans who answered the call for more coal included brothers Hobart and Wilbur McNeill, who started the Iowa Central Coal Company in 1873 in the Muchakinock Creek valley about four miles south of Oskaloosa. While the McNeills bought other coal mines and merged them to become the Consolidation Coal Company in 1875, the town that began growing on their property was named after the nearby creek.

The McNeills sold their company in 1881 to the Chicago and North Western Railroad, which wanted a dependable supply of coal. Able to operate independently of the railroad, Consolidation's board of directors knew that if they provided good living and working conditions, their employees would reward the company with good work. Most of the credit goes to Consolidation's first general superintendent, John E. Buxton, and his son and successor Ben. Just as the C&NWRR wanted a reliable source of coal, the Buxtons wanted a steady workforce, and they began recruiting African Americans in Virginia, who responded eagerly.

In June 1883, "Muchy" had 1,200 residents, with almost two-thirds of them blacks. The largest non-black group were Swedes, followed by British, Welsh and Scottish miners. Black professionals were also recruited to come to Muchakinock, which became called the "colored Athens of Iowa."

Blacks and whites worked in the mines and company offices and supported all the businesses; socially some stayed apart, although nothing has ever indicated racial tensions existed there. Hobe Armstrong, a black businessman and community leader, suggested the races would get along better by intermarrying, something he advocated to his children, who all married whites. By 1895, Muchy had 3,844 people. Even though about a quarter of the population was black at this time, Muchy still had a reputation as a black town.

Although Iowa was the fifth-leading state in the production of coal in 1890, the veins of coal around Muchakinock were thinning. At the decade's end, Consolidation started to build a town near three new mines ten miles to the southwest. Ben Buxton planned the new community, named after his father, to have about fifty blocks laid out in a grid that was more orderly than Muchakinock had been.

As soon as homes were built in Buxton in 1900, Consolidation arranged for the families in Muchy to move into them without regard to race. Slowly, the new town began to fill.

Putting Buxton on top of a hill assured the town of good drainage, something most mining towns rarely had. Poor drainage caused diseases to spread. The company built each family a well-constructed, one-and-a-half story, six-room house. They had wood floors, and the interiors were plastered. An outhouse was behind every home. The company hauled water to the houses daily. Coal sheds were next to the alleys so the crews of horse-drawn wagons could put coal in them without going on anyone's property. Families had stoves for cooking and heating. They could plant their own vegetable, fruit and flower gardens. Space was made for families' chickens, cows and hogs. The company planted trees in the neighborhoods and created parks. Athletic teams and bands formed. At least seventeen churches went up.

Hearing good things about Consolidation's business ethics and its new town, more people from other areas moved there. By 1905, 2,700 blacks and 1,991 whites were living near each other there. Although a company town, Buxton did not require its employees to live there. Families could lease or purchase acreage in other areas owned by the company and build their own houses on those lands. The residents were not required to purchase supplies at the company store, which was so large it had 135 clerks. Indeed, about forty businesses not connected with Consolidation were established in the downtown and in another commercial district. Buxton had meat markets, five restaurants, groceries, three barbershops, bakers, drugstores, tailors, a shoe store, a hotel, a hardware store and a dance hall, among other businesses.

Fifteen black miners did double duty—after being in the mines during the day, they worked at their own laundry and bakery at night. Whatever could be found in a big city could be bought in Buxton—phonograph records, Stetson hats and fine dresses and suits. What couldn't be bought in town could be mail-ordered. Farmers who lived a distance from Buxton brought their eggs and produce to sell because they were paid more than in other towns. One young black girl who grew up there said, "In Buxton, you didn't have to want for nothing."

Noting that residents of railroad towns appreciated the YMCAs their owners built for them, Consolidation erected a three-story YMCA in Buxton in 1903. The auditorium on its second floor could hold one thousand people. At first it was for blacks only, but then whites were admitted to events, too. An addition held a swimming pool. One black man said, years after living in Buxton, "It was the black man's Utopia."

A black woman who had lived in Buxton later said she never knew what segregation meant until she moved away.

People who lived in Buxton said that while the races worked side by side, they did not socialize that much. They also said Consolidation cracked down on discrimination and removed those who disrespected others. When violence occurred, it was more on a personal than a racial level and usually within each racial group.

If anyone thinks other coal mine towns were like Buxton, blacks and whites living in harmony because they had to work together, the answer is no. In most other mining towns, they lived in separate neighborhoods, with the blacks generally living on the outskirts of town in smaller, older and more run-down housing compared to the white workers. Schools were segregated, churches, theaters and public spaces too. Blacks could not enter their company towns' hotels and restaurants. Newspapers in those towns promoted their companies' beliefs, but not so in Buxton, where four newspapers published what they wanted.

By 1910, mining coal was full throttle in Iowa. About eighteen thousand miners were working in the state. Buxton now had about six thousand residents, although reportedly up to ten thousand people lived there and in smaller neighboring communities much like suburbs. It was the largest coal mining community west of the Mississippi.

Around the end of World War I, when demand for coal was high, Buxton miners earned ten dollars a day, an unheard-of salary at the time.

Unfortunately, with mining towns, when the reason they were created disappears, they disappear, too. A cascade of events fell on Buxton. The coal there became harder to find, and what was found didn't compare to better grades of coal being mined in the eastern states. During World War I, Consolidation opened two mines that were ten and eighteen miles west of Buxton and set up camp towns for them. Some Buxton families moved to those places. An explosion closed a shaft near Buxton, putting three hundred miners out of business. The C&NWRR found it cheaper to buy coal from private sources than its own subsidiary. Fires in 1916 and 1917 destroyed several businesses in Buxton that never rebuilt. The remaining mine at Buxton closed in 1918. Families continued to leave for new mines. Consolidation sold out to another company, which itself moved away. By 1927, Buxton was finished.

Practically nothing of Buxton remains, just woods and farm fields. All that indicates that Buxton existed is a historical sign on the north edge of Lovilia, five miles west of where the most integrated town in the United States stood.

In 1938, an expert on Iowa's coal industry said enough coal was under the state to last three thousand years. However, the last coal mine in the state closed in 1991.

OTTUMWA

Canteen in the Alley

Nearly every town has an institution, and in Ottumwa, that's Canteen Lunch, both in its appearance—a low, rectangular yellow-brick building that was built during the Depression—and its menu, which seems to have changed little over the years. That's a good thing, many people say. It opened in 1927 as a five-seat diner in another location but, after nine years, moved to its current site. A chance to move again, unwillingly, came in the 1970s when the city wanted to build a parking lot here—meaning Canteen Lunch would have to go—but people raised such a fuss that city officials let the diner alone. Instead, the parking ramp was built around it. So here it stands with sixteen stools lining an oval counter.

The menu is limited: a loose-meat sandwich with and without cheese, fried egg on a bun and a hot dog. The usual lineup of soft drinks is here along with coffee, tea, root beer floats and six flavors of malts and shakes. The sixteen types of homemade pies here include apple and strawberry rhubarb to pecan, wildberry and raisin cream, which can be topped with ice cream. Nothing highfalutin is at this place, and apparently that's just fine with those who eat here.

Despite having "lunch" in its title, Canteen Lunch is open from midmorning until early evening, Monday through Saturday.

PELLA

Dutch Letters

Jaarsma Bakery in Pella has been making foods and pastries since 1898, in particular the S letters made of eggs, butter, flour and almond paste.

When immigrant Harmon Jaarsma opened his bakery in 1898, he specialized in Dutch foods. Among the traditional fare he and his help made in the wood-fired brick ovens were Dutch letters, a tradition that continues through today. These pastries, made of eggs, flour and butter, stuffed with almond paste and sprinkled with sugar, were originally made only during the Christmas holidays in the Netherlands. The S letters represented Sinterklaas, the Dutch Santa Claus. However, the S was so popular that Jaarsma began making them throughout the year, not just at Christmas. Jaarsma concentrated on making the curvy letters since they're easier to make than many other letters that have joints.

The fourth generation of the founder's family now runs Jaarsma Bakery, on the south side of Pella's main square. Approximately two thousand S letters are made daily, and during the city's three-day Tulip Time Festival each spring, about forty-two thousand are made. Besides the letters, Jaarsma makes apple bread, krackling, goat legs (chocolate-covered almond cookies), Dutch spice cookies called speculaas and many other cakes, cookies and rolls derived from Dutch recipes.

Scholte House

In 1847, forty-two-year-old Hendrik Pieter Scholte led several hundred followers of his ministry from Holland to settle in Iowa. Like other groups that immigrated to the United States, they left their native country because they were suffering economically and, having split from the state-sponsored church in the 1830s, were persecuted for their beliefs. At various times, Scholte had been sentenced to prison, fined and, according to him, stoned by religious opponents. The decision to move to Iowa had been planned for some years. The group even had a name for their new home: Pella, which is Hebrew for "a city of refuge."

Scholte's group had planned to travel to the United States with members led by another minister, but that group left earlier and settled the city of Holland, Michigan, in March 1847 instead of going to Iowa as planned. Scholte's followers crossed the Atlantic a month later on four sailing ships. However, Scholte, who had inherited wealth, traveled on the *Caledonia*, one of the first sailboats to also use stream-driven paddlewheels. That ship put Scholte, his second wife (his first died in 1844) and his family in Boston after a voyage of only thirteen days. His followers, however, needed up to eight weeks to cross the ocean.

In June, Scholte and his followers arrived in St. Louis. Not long afterward, Scholte and four men made an exploratory trip to Iowa to secure land for everyone. In Fairfield, they met a Baptist minister who had traveled the area since 1841 while doing double duty as a mail carrier, and he guided them to a rise in the prairie about five miles east of the Des Moines River in Marion County. Offering $1.25 per acre to the settlers who were already there, Scholte and his advance party bought eighteen thousand acres for those to follow them. They also arranged for cabins to be built for his people.

Knowing all eight hundred followers would find it hard to live on the frontier at this time, six hundred or so were chosen to go to Pella in August 1847. The rest, who would take temporary housing and jobs in St. Louis, would follow the next year. Unfortunately, the men who had agreed to build the log cabins for the first group failed to do so. That forced the new arrivals to do the best they could. Some bought the few log cabins the settlers had left behind. Others made sod houses for themselves. Because the earthen roofs were often covered with straw, Pella was nicknamed "Strawtown" by some. Generally, the sod houses were okay for a while, but in at least one case, a cow attracted to the grass growing on top of a soddy was too heavy for its

Hendrik Pieter Scholte, the founder of Pella, completed this home for his family in 1848. The house has up to thirty rooms, depending on who is counting.

roof to bear and fell into the room below. No one, or the cow, was hurt, just surprised, say the records.

After choosing a parcel of land, Scholte began erecting a house that same year for himself and his family. Made of black walnut, oak and stone from the area, it was one of the first buildings in the town he had already platted, and in April 1848, the Scholte family moved from a log cabin into the new house. Rather than reflecting the heritage of buildings seen in Holland, the house was designed in the Greek Revival style then popular in the United States. Scholte's wife, Maria, ordered wallpaper, furniture and carpeting for the house. Some of the wallpaper is said to still be in the house. The house was added onto and its construction altered several times since it was built.

Now, the house has twelve exterior doors and forty-one more inside, plus six sets of stairs. It has twenty-six to thirty rooms, depending on how a person defines them. The library is the only room that exists as the Scholtes decorated it. In 1979, the house was deeded over to the Pella Historical Society, although the last descendant of the builders lived in it until 1987.

Van Spanckeren Rowhouse and Earp Home

East of downtown Pella is the Pella Historical Village, a compilation of original structures, buildings moved to the site and replicas, the biggest of which is the twelve-story-tall windmill that looms above the town. The part above the windmill's brick wall was built in Holland for the village, disassembled and shipped to Pella, where it was reassembled in 2002.

One original structure, which remains where it was built around 1855, is a two-unit row house with a common wall separating the units. Brothers B.H. and J.H.H. Van Spanckeren, who had arrived with other members of their family in Pella in the late 1840s, built the house. Because it was built with tie rods providing structural support for the floors, it's considered one of the better examples of Dutch architecture in the nation.

The east unit at 505 Franklin Street was owned by B.H., who started a bakery elsewhere in town and later turned that into a general store around 1873. J.H.H. had his tailor shop on the first floor at 507 Franklin Street and lived upstairs.

In 1850, Nicholas and Virginia Earp, who had Scottish and English ancestries, bought a farm seven miles northeast of Pella after moving here with their children Newton, James, Virgil and Wyatt. Named after an army officer Nicholas admired during the Mexican-American War, Wyatt was then two years old.

Nicholas sold the farm because of financial difficulties in 1856, and the family moved back and forth between Pella and Monmouth, Illinois, for the next few years. Residing in Pella most of the Civil War, they lived at 505 Franklin Street on the ground floor while owner B.H. Van Spanckeren accessed his quarters on the second floor by exterior stairs.

Wyatt's older brothers joined the Union army, and Nicholas worked as a recruiter in Pella. Wyatt ran away three times to join the army, but his father brought him home each time. During the years in Pella, the family grew with four more children: Morgan in 1851, Baxter in 1855, Virginia in 1858 and Adelia in 1861.

In 1864, Nicholas led a wagon train of eleven families to California. From there the Earps went various ways, geographically and otherwise. Before Wyatt gained fame as a lawman, he was charged with operating and visiting brothels and was jailed briefly for being a horse thief but broke out of jail. Wyatt worked on the Transcontinental Railroad and migrated in early 1874 to Wichita, Kansas, where James owned a brothel. Wyatt may have been a bouncer. After helping a police officer find wagon thieves, Wyatt became a

Wichita policeman in April 1875. A year later, he was fired for getting into a fistfight that had political overtones.

James left to open another brothel in Dodge City, and once more, Wyatt followed, with a seven-month interlude selling firewood in Deadwood, Dakota Territory. Returning to Dodge City, he became an assistant marshal in May 1878 and, two months later, mortally wounded a cowhand who had shot up a saloon.

In 1879, Virgil Earp, now a law officer in Prescott, Arizona Territory, suggested to Wyatt, Morgan and James they join him. On December 1 of that year, Wyatt and James accompanied Virgil to his new posting as assistant U.S. marshal at the silver mining town of Tombstone, which then had one thousand residents. Morgan arrived the following July, and two months later Wyatt's friend John Henry "Doc" Holliday came to town.

During their time in Tombstone, Virgil Earp and those with him had run-ins with members of what were called Cowboys, a pejorative name at the time for area outlaws. Legitimate cattlemen were called herders, drovers and ranchers.

Confrontations between the two groups came to a head in an empty lot near the back end of Tombstone's OK Corral on October 26, 1881. After about thirty seconds and thirty bullets, three of the six Cowboys at the scene were killed. Holliday was bruised by a bullet striking his holster, Morgan was wounded in the thigh and Virgil hit by bullet that tore across his shoulder blades and struck his vertebrae. Wyatt was untouched. James Earp also lived in Tombstone at the time but was not involved in the gunfight.

Following an inquiry that absolved the Earps and Holliday of murder, unknown assailants wounded Virgil and assassinated Morgan in separate incidents over the next few months. Dissatisfied because the attackers were never tried, Wyatt formed a posse of his younger brother Warren, Holliday and three others in March 1882 to go on what was called a vendetta ride and killed four more of the Cowboys.

After that, Earp left Arizona Territory and wandered through western states and jobs for nearly the rest of his life. He gambled at cards, bought and sold horses, refereed boxing matches, got into mining again, tried to sell gold-painted rocks to rubes, defused a property-line dispute and jumped a few claims. Even at six feet tall and at least 165 pounds, he also jockeyed racing horses. Then he owned a San Diego saloon where his gambling games earned him $1,000 a night; lived in Alaska for two years where he made a living by, in his words, "mining the miners"; operated another saloon there, which, again, had a brothel; illegally brought back criminals from Mexico to

Los Angeles; and acted as a consultant with western silent movies. He met director John Ford and another Iowan—a young prop boy named Marion Morrison, who later became known as John Wayne.

Wyatt died in January 1929 at the age of eighty in Los Angeles. Friends from Tombstone and Alaska attended his funeral along with early western movie stars Tom Mix and William S. Hart. His widow had his body cremated and buried in a cemetery in Colma, California. He was the last of the Earp brothers and the last participant in the OK Corral gunfight to die.

WINTERSET

Covered Bridges

The covered bridges in Madison County were well known and had attracted tourists for years before Robert James Waller (1939–2017) wrote his 1992 novel *The Bridges of Madison County*. His book and the 1995 movie of the same name that stars Clint Eastwood and Meryl Streep just made them more famous.

They were built like boxes to shelter the wooden decks from rain, snow and ice. The county officials who ordered the wooden bridges to be built considered the costs of replacing the sides and tops of the bridges to be far cheaper than the heavy boards that made up the decks. Many covered bridges were painted red like barns with white ends to increase visibility as people approached them.

The first covered bridge in Iowa was erected at Fort Des Moines in 1844, where downtown Des Moines is now. Up to fifty covered bridges were built in twenty-five of Iowa's ninety-nine counties. Madison County's first covered bridge was built in 1868 by Eli Cox, and it lasted until replaced by a conventional bridge in 1913. At least eighteen more covered bridges were built in Madison County, the greatest number of such bridges in any Iowa county. Some were washed away in floods, and others were removed as safety hazards. Arson has also hit the bridges. In 1986, a man wanting to remove the carved initials of a failed relationship ended up burning down the McBride Bridge.

Now, just six covered bridges remain in Madison County, all within eleven miles of Winterset, the county seat. Imes Bridge, built in 1870, was the second covered bridge built in the county and is the oldest of those

Built in 1884, Hogback Bridge was one of nearly twenty covered bridges that existed in Madison County. Now, just six remain, all within a few miles of Winterset.

still standing. Others include Cutler-Donahoe, Holliwell, Cedar, Roseman and Hogback, which was the last built, in 1884. All were renovated during the 1990s, particularly with their increased popularity. Roseman Bridge was the principal site in the book, but Holliwell stood in for it during the filming of the movie.

In 2002, an unknown arsonist torched Cedar Bridge, but it was rebuilt. Similarly, the 1880 farmhouse used in the movie as the home of Francesca Johnson, the farm wife Streep plays, was set afire but not destroyed in 2003. No one has been charged in that crime.

In 2017, arsonists again destroyed Cedar Bridge. The three teenage arsonists were ordered to pay restitution and given suspended sentences. The rebuilt bridge was opened in 2019 and is the only one of the bridges that vehicles can use.

Winterset holds the Madison County Covered Bridge Festival on the second full weekend of each October. A few other original covered bridges remain in Iowa, three in Marion County and one in southeast Polk County.

John Wayne Birthplace

Actor John Wayne, whose movie career covered about forty years around the middle of the twentieth century, is remembered mostly for his portrayals of cowboys of the early American West. Yet he came from solid midwestern roots. Weighing thirteen pounds, he was born Marion Robert Morrison on May 30, 1907, in a back room of this small, white-painted house in Winterset. The house is decorated much like it would have been when he lived there with his parents.

Marion was the first child of Clyde Morrison, a Winterset pharmacist, and Mary "Molly" Brown Morrison, a telephone operator in Des Moines, who provided their son with English, Scottish and Irish ancestry. Three years later, they moved to Earlham, about twelve miles away but still close to both sets of the couple's parents. In 1911, they had another son and wanting to call him Robert, they changed their firstborn's name to Marion Mitchell Morrison, the name of his grandfather who had been wounded in the Civil War and carried saber wounds and a bullet in his head until he died in 1915.

Clyde and Molly Morrison moved their family to southern California in 1916. A local fireman, who noticed young Marion walking near his fire station often with the family's Airedale terrier, Duke, nicknamed the young boy "Little Duke" and the nickname stuck, though evolving ultimately into "Duke" throughout his life. Later, Morrison became a prop boy and film extra for movie director John Ford. He appeared in at least twenty movies without credit or as Marion Morrison.

When film director Raoul Walsh met Morrison, he suggested a name change. Liking the name of Revolutionary War hero Mad Anthony Wayne, Walsh turned Marion Morrison into John Wayne for the 1930 movie *The Big Trail*.

Wayne became a star when Ford cast him as the lead, Ringo Kid, in the 1939 movie *Stagecoach*. Of all his roles, it was playing a drunken, overweight, one-eyed sheriff in the 1969 movie *True Grit* that earned Wayne an Oscar for Best Actor. Although he starred in, produced and directed at least 142 movies, he never legally changed his name to John Wayne. On all his passports, he remained Marion Mitchell Morrison.

The house is part of the John Wayne Birthplace Museum, which opened in 2015. Its 6,100-square-foot building has collections of memorabilia relating to Wayne's roles in the movies (the eyepatch he wore in *True Grit* was actually see-through so he could watch what others were doing on the sets) and artifacts from his private life and relationships with other actors of his day.

7

NORTHEAST IOWA

BURR OAK

Masters Hotel/Laura Ingalls Wilder Park and Museum

People familiar with the *Little House* books penned by Laura Ingalls Wilder know that she wrote about practically every place she lived while growing up in the Midwest, with one exception: Burr Oak, Iowa. She lived there when her parents, Charles and Caroline Ingalls, began managing an eleven-room hotel in Burr Oak in October 1876 for family friends William and Mary Steadman. The Steadmans had just purchased it from William Masters, who had bought it in 1873. It had been built in 1856, which makes it one of the oldest extant hotels in Iowa.

When the Ingallses were here, Burr Oak was a stagecoach stop. The hotel's first floor had a barroom, parlors, a bedroom for the five members of the Steadman family and another bedroom for a long-term occupant. Four more bedrooms were on the second floor, and one of those was also for another long-term occupant. Travelers sometimes slept three to a bed at twenty-five cents each.

The Ingallses—Charles, Caroline, Laura and her sisters Mary and Carrie—lived in the basement with a kitchen-bedroom and a dining room. Another daughter, Grace, was born here in May 1877.

Caroline cooked for visitors while Charles managed the place. He also worked at a mill since the Steadmans paid them no salary. The older children helped with chores and meals. Laura later wrote, "Ma was always tired; Pa was always busy."

Even though the Ingallses had a barroom in the hotel, they did not like the rough goings-on at the next-door saloon. Relations between the Steadmans and Ingalls family deteriorated, and after three months, the Ingallses moved into an apartment elsewhere in Burr Oak. Then they rented a house. Sometime in August or September 1877, the Ingallses left town in the middle of the night for Walnut Grove, Minnesota. Charles had debts in Burr Oak when they left there, but he made good on them later.

In August 1885, Laura married Almanzo Wilder and settled on a farm at Mansfield, Missouri, in 1894. There, she began her writing career with a Missouri publication in 1911.

Still, it wasn't until 1932 that Laura collaborated with her forty-six-year-old daughter, Rose Wilder Lane, to publish the first of the *Little House* books.

Laura died in 1957 and was buried in Mansfield next to Almanzo, who died in 1949. Rose was buried near them in 1968.

Beginning in the 1970s, Burr Oak residents restored what's still called the Masters Hotel to how it appeared when the Ingallses were there. A set of embroidered handkerchiefs and glassware owned by Laura are displayed here along with items relating to her writings.

CEDAR FALLS

Ice House Museum

As early as 1858, Cedar Falls had an icehouse where the Ice House Museum now stands to take advantage of the ice that formed on the Cedar River a few steps away. When Hugh Smith built this one in 1921, he used hollow clay tile to form the one-hundred-foot-diameter building that was thirty feet high and could hold sixteen million pounds of ice.

Sawdust and straw insulated the slabs of ice, which were used to chill or freeze meats and other foods. Some ice was used to cool drinks and desserts. Ice wagons delivered blocks of ice to customers. Many families used ice to keep perishables cool in the wood-and-metal ice boxes that began appearing as early as the 1820s and became more practical for home use in the middle of the nineteenth century.

The demand for ice grew until early modern refrigerators appeared in the second decade of the twentieth century. That slowly crushed the ice industry.

In 1934, the icehouse closed, and the building went through several uses. The city and the Cedar Falls Historical Society then worked to preserve the building and opened it in 1979 as the Ice House Museum, the nation's only icehouse museum in its original building.

CLAYTON COUNTY

Cassville Ferry

The Cassville Ferry began operating in 1833, when Iowa and Wisconsin were not yet states, crossing the Mississippi River between Cassville, Wisconsin, and a landing just south of where the Turkey River meets the larger river. The Cassville Ferry is the last ferry connected with Iowa. All those that were within the state—at Keokuk, Dubuque, Council Bluffs, Cedar Rapids, Massillon and perhaps a few more places—are long gone. Also, the Cassville Ferry is the oldest operating ferry in Wisconsin.

Two five-hundred-horsepower diesel engines propel the tug *The Pride of Cassville*, which was made in 2008 for the City of Cassville, which operates the ferry. At the same time, a new barge that holds 150 people and twelve vehicles during the fifteen-minute rides was also purchased. In 2016, the ferry carried 25,141 people and 9,435 vehicles. (Floods have affected data from more recent years.)

The ferry is the only way to cross the Mississippi between Marquette and Dubuque, eighty-five miles apart. A solar-powered call box on the Iowa side can summon the May-through-October ferry, as can calling the tug's office in the Cassville City Hall at 608-725-5180.

CLERMONT

Montauk

Born in Ledyard, Connecticut, in 1832, William Larrabee moved to Iowa in 1853 to work as a teacher. After one year of teaching, he went to work on his brother-in-law's 2,100-acre farm in Allamakee County. He also purchased an interest in 1856 in a Clermont grain mill and bought out the others three years later. Likewise, he began buying land in northeast Iowa, eventually amassing more than 200,000 acres in his lifetime. In April 1861, he married Anna Matilda Appelman, who was also from Ledyard and whose father was a sea captain. The Larrabees had nine children between 1862 and 1876.

Larrabee tried to enlist in the Union army during the Civil War but was rejected because he had lost an eye due to a gun accident while in his teens. Unfit for combat, he nonetheless gave free flour to the families of soldiers fighting in the war.

Two years after the war, he became an Iowa state senator for eighteen years and advocated the expansion of railroads in Iowa, but he also worked to keep them from financially exploiting citizens.

In 1874, construction began on the two-story, fourteen-room mansion that Anna Larrabee called Montauk after a lighthouse on the east end of Long Island, New York, that had guided her seafaring father home many times. Montauk's bricks were made of locally fired clays, and stone for its foundation was quarried in the area. Built on a two-hundred-foot-tall hill, the house was the centerpiece of the Larrabees' seventy-four-acre farm where chickens, peacocks, hogs and turkeys were raised along with cattle—the Larrabees were among the first to raise Brown Swiss cattle in Iowa. A garden and orchard furnished vegetables and fruits, including about three hundred pounds of grapes a year. A creamery, combination windmill–water tower, caretaker's house, laundry, barn, icehouse, workshop and carriage were among the buildings on the grounds. More than 100,000 trees were planted on the estate, and thirty-seven acres were set aside for crops.

While architect E. Townsend Mix wanted conventional fireplaces, Larrabee preferred steam heat to warm the house, and the two men compromised. Fireplaces were installed but never used, as the coal-fired steam heat system proved more practical. Each bedroom had its own bathroom with a marble sink and running water. Because Larrabee had a fear of fire, each room had two doors and a fire extinguisher.

Statuettes by Ferdinando Vici and the Pugi brothers of Italy were selected for the interior, while outside were bronze statues honoring Civil War heroes: U.S. Grant, William Sherman, Grenville Dodge and David Farragut.

Larrabee purchased paintings by famous artists of his day, including John George Brown and William Bradford, who was known for his seascapes. One painting, *Stormy Weather* by Peter Molyn, dates to 1670. Upstairs is a

Left: William Larrabee named his mansion Montauk after a Long Island, New York lighthouse when he built it in the 1870s. Larrabee served as Iowa's governor from 1886 to 1890.

Below: The huge Patent Wooten desk is the centerpiece of William Larrabee's study in Montauk. Almost everything in the state historic site was owned by the Larrabee family.

half-finished painting—Larrabee's daughter Augusta died at the age of thirty-two before finishing the portrait of her husband of seven months.

The library on the main floor has countless books and some rare items, including a life-mask of a clean-shaven Abraham Lincoln, a revolving bookcase and a massive Wooten desk that opens to reveal a warren of drawers, cubbyholes, shelves and a fold-down writing desk. An early model of a typewriter with upper- and lowercase keys is here— Larrabee bought it to use after learning that others could not decipher his penmanship.

Larrabee insisted all meals be formal, and none of the children ate with the parents until they knew how to behave and take part in conversations. When the daughters played the Mason-Hamlin piano in the music room, their father accompanied them on a cello. The family also had Tiffany lamps, Swiss music boxes and a small French-made mechanical bird in the parlor.

Larrabee loved to keep up with the times, installing a phone in 1900 and then, in 1910, electricity. He bought one of Thomas Edison's phonographs to teach himself Spanish from a record before he made a trip to Cuba.

Compared to historic homes that feature furnishings that approximate what may have been in them decades ago, everything in Montauk is original—not replacements or reproductions—and this is a lot of what makes Montauk so special. It must be one of the most complete nineteenth-century historic homes open to the public.

In 1885, Larrabee, one of the richest men in the Midwest, was elected to the first of two two-year terms as governor of Iowa. Afterward, he retired to Montauk, although he remained quite a traveler—making long trips to Europe and Palestine—and chaired the Iowa exhibit at the St. Louis World's Fair. He also was a confidant of President Teddy Roosevelt.

Governor Larrabee died in 1912 and his wife in 1931. Their last surviving child, also named Anna, kept the house and everything in it intact. She died there at the age of ninety-six in 1965, and the house was opened to the public two years later. It is now a state historic site.

Union Sunday School

In 1863, Presbyterians in Clermont built a church in town but gave it up when their congregation folded five years later. The nondenominational Union Sunday School, which had been meeting in a private home in Clermont, then began using the building. As members, the Larrabees started a lending library there in 1877 and donated the world's largest Kimball pipe organ to the school in 1896. The organ was restored in 2010 and is played for special occasions.

DECORAH

Seed Savers Exchange

In 1975, Diane Ott Whealy's grandfather presented her with what may have seemed like any other tomato and morning glory seeds, but these were different, having been brought from Bavaria by his father. To Diane and her husband, Kent, they were heirlooms, seeds of plants found nowhere else in North America.

When the Whealys learned others were interested in preserving, growing and sharing seeds, they formed Seed Savers Exchange for those people to communicate with one another. Now, Seed Savers Exchange has more than twenty thousand varieties in its long-term storage called the seed bank. Because no seed can last forever, the nonprofit organization grows and renews several hundred varieties at its Heritage Farm. Among the plants it keeps are flowers, vegetables, grains, herbs and spices.

Among the historic seeds (ones grown before 1950) that Seed Savers Exchange offers is Selzer Purple radish, an early-maturing annual that was brought from Germany in 1867 to the Amana Colonies. The Connecticut Wonder Bean came about when bees near Bolton, Connecticut, cross-pollinated two types of beans in 1919. Willard Collards Greens, which grow

Plants from throughout the years are grown from the more than twenty thousand types of seeds preserved at Seed Savers Exchange north of Decorah.

up to three feet across (twice the normal size), were grown in North Carolina in the 1920s and handed down through the generations of one family. The Talent Tomato seeds have come down from a single tomato that was observed growing more vigorously than the Medford tomatoes at Ashland, Oregon, in the 1960s. Of course, Seed Savers Exchange has the German Pink Tomato seeds given to Diane Ott Whealy by her grandfather.

About six thousand types of seeds are sold annually through its catalogue and website or at its store at the show gardens, which are six miles north of Decorah.

Highlandville School

Sometimes mistaken as a church because of its bell tower, Highlandville School was built in 1911 as a two-room schoolhouse. A wall with pocket doors, usually shut during classes, separated the rooms. One was used for kindergarten through fourth grade students, the other for fifth through eighth grades. Older students went to a high school seven miles to the west.

For occasions such as plays, musicals, elections and dances, the desks were pushed aside, and the pocket doors slid into the walls to create a large open area. After classes ceased in 1964, the schoolhouse continued to be used for events as before.

Highlandville School turns into a dance hall when the Foot-Notes, a local group that has played in the Kennedy Center for Performing Arts, and other musicians play there. The schoolhouse is open during the warm months only, and just as it was way back then, visitors use the nearby outhouses.

Anyone wanting to visit inside the school can pick up a key at the Highland General Store, a short walk away and a story in itself.

ELKADER

Motor Mill

In the late 1860s, John Thompson and others formed a company to build a mill alongside the river at the town of Motor, four miles southeast of Elkader, the county seat. The six-story mill was made of locally quarried stone at a cost of $90,000, which included the milling equipment. Each of the mill's four walls has a unique appearance because each was made by a different stonemason. No nails were used in the timber framework and floors. A stone house, stables and icehouse were built too.

When finished in 1869, the mill ground everything—wheat, buckwheat, corn, barley, rye and oats.

In the 1890s, following a flood, lack of a railroad, crop losses and more, the mill closed. For eighty years, the site was a farm, and the mill was used to store grains and provide shelter for horses.

In 1985, the Clayton County Conservation Board acquired the property and turned it into a 155-acre park, a picturesque spot alongside the Maquoketa River. Free tours of the mill are given weekend afternoons from Memorial Day through mid-October.

FESTINA

St. Anthony of Padua Chapel

When Johann Gaertner went off to fight for Napoleon in battles including Moscow and Waterloo, his mother promised to build a chapel to honor him and dedicate it to the Virgin Mary. When he returned home safe after the wars, she never completed her promise. Ultimately, he moved to northeast Iowa and built the chapel himself.

When he died in June 1887 at the age of ninety-three, Gaertner was laid to rest here. He's said to be the only member of Napoleon's army to be buried in Iowa. At sixteen by twenty feet and only able to hold eight to ten worshippers, the stone chapel is one of the smallest churches in the world. Topped by a forty-foot-high steeple, the St. Anthony of Padua Chapel is less than three miles west of Festina on gravel roads.

FORT ATKINSON

Fort Atkinson State Preserve

While many forts in the United States were built to protect the westward-moving populations of European Americans from Native Americans, Fort

Atkinson had a unique purpose. It was built to keep factions of Native Americans from fighting each other. In 1825, the U.S. government created a boundary line between the Dakota to the north of the line and the allied Sac and Fox (Sauk and Meskwaki) to the south. This line ran from northeast Iowa in a southwesterly direction for two hundred miles. Unfortunately, a line on a map didn't mean a thing to the warring tribes. To remedy the situation, the government created a neutral zone that was forty miles wide and straddled the boundary.

None of the Dakota or Sac and Fox was to live within this zone. Rather, the United States was forcing a third tribe, the Winnebago (Ho-Chunk), off its lands in Wisconsin to move into the neutral zone. Although the Winnebago were on good terms with the opponents, they were apprehensive about being placed between them. As an enticement to go along with the plan, each tribe was given cash, and the government agreed to build Fort Atkinson for troops to maintain the peace. The troops were also to keep the Winnebago from going back to Wisconsin.

In 1840, three years of construction began on Fort Atkinson (named after its commander Henry Atkinson) on a hill overlooking the Turkey River. Half of the troops enforced the neutral zone, and half worked on constructing the fort's twenty-four buildings of locally quarried limestone and wood. They also built a wooden palisade that was eleven feet, nine inches tall around the fort.

With white settlers wanting more and more land, including in Iowa, the Winnebago, Dakota, Sac and Fox in northeast Iowa were moved again, in stages from 1846 to 1853, to places far to the west. When the need for the fort disappeared, it was abandoned in 1849.

Half of a stone barracks has been restored, as have some other buildings and part of the stockade wall. An 1840s-style rendezvous is held at the preserve on the last full weekend of each September.

FROELICH

Froelich Foundation

Case IH, Massey Ferguson, New Holland and John Deere are names long associated with farm tractors, yet the one name most responsible for gasoline-powered tractors is little known—John Froehlich.

Froelich (pronounced FRAY-lich) was born in Illinois in 1849 and moved to the village of Froelich, which was settled by his German immigrant parents. That same year also was the birth of a new application of steam power—the farm tractor. Steam had been used on farms since around 1818 when stationary engines were set in fields to power equipment there. After a while, they were put on horse-drawn wagons that could move them where needed. That contrivance gave way in 1849 to a steam-powered engine that could drive itself into fields and operate equipment there.

However, these self-propelled engines were heavy, weighing twenty to thirty thousand pounds. The heaviest weighed sixty-eight thousand pounds. Yet horses remained—needed to pull wagons carrying fuel and water to the steam engines in the fields.

In the 1880s, South Dakota farmers would hire threshing crews to harvest their crops, and Froelich had been heading one of those crews, a sixteen-man outfit that used steam-powered tractors. Like other threshers, they learned South Dakota had little wood to burn in the tractors. Some crews used coal, but that also had to be hauled into the fields. Either way, a steam engine consumed about a ton of wood or coal a day. Sometimes Froelich's crew burned straw to heat the water, and water was a problem too. A typical steam engine would use up to 1,500 gallons of water a day. Unfortunately, most of the water in South Dakota was alkaline, which proved corrosive to many components in the steam engines. Also, harvesting crews needed a long time to heat the water hot enough to boil. At the end of a day, a steam tractor would harvest about a thousand bushels of wheat.

Froelich had known about gasoline-powered engines and, having used one to power some well-drilling equipment, thought they would work better in the fields than the steam engines. In 1892, he and a friend, blacksmith and mechanic William Mann, set out to create the first gasoline-powered tractor with forward and reverse gears.

Upon visiting the gas-engine manufacturing firm Van Duzen Company of Cincinnati, Ohio, Froelich purchased one of its one-cylinder, sixteen-horsepower gas engines. Back in Iowa, after removing the engine and other gear from a steam-driven tractor, he and Mann created a gasoline-powered tractor with the Van Duzen engine. This was no matter of simply removing one engine and replacing it with another. The men had to fabricate new shafts, numerous gears and many more parts to seat the new engine and attach it to drive the rear wheels forward and backward. At nine thousand pounds, Froelich's invention was lighter than steam tractors. Also, it started just by cranking a handle.

The gas tank was set high so gravity would drop the fuel through a pipe to the engine. A round steering wheel stood atop a steel column at the very front of the tractor, and the driver would stand there on a platform of wooden boards when operating the machine. Exposed chains connected the steering mechanism to the front wheels. Leather belts, wide or narrow, ran endless loops, transferring energy between sets of mechanical wheels. Spinning flywheels whirled dangerously close to the operator. Gear teeth moved so quickly they were blurs. Today's OSHA inspectors would call it a nightmare.

To conserve water, Froelich and Mann designed a system that recirculated water to draw heat off the engine. It then would cool down when run through a primitive type of radiator. At the end of a day, Froelich's invention would use just a barrel of water and twenty-six gallons of gasoline.

After testing the tractor on a neighbor's field with good results, Froelich and a threshing crew put it on a train that took them to South Dakota that fall. There, they ran it for fifty-two days, producing seventy-two thousand bushels of grain.

Upon his return, Froelich met with businessmen in Waterloo, and they formed the Waterloo Gasoline Traction Engine Company. After a few years, he left the company, which was then bought in 1918 by Deere & Company, a farm implement manufacturer. That business evolved into the John Deere Tractor Company, which used Froelich's tractor as the prototype for its popular Waterloo Boy Tractor. In a few decades, steam tractors were no more.

The John Froelich Foundation maintains the site of where Froelich lived and invented his gas-powered tractor. The original disappeared long ago, but a half-scale model of it is in the blacksmith shop. Also here is what's called the Iron Clad Store, an 1891 general store–post office that had an iron exterior to keep the building safe from sparks given off by trains on the nearby tracks. An 1866 school is also here along with a 1907 barn and a reproduction of a train depot. The site has an annual festival of old tractors and more on the last full weekend of September.

By the time Froelich died in 1933, he held fourteen patents.

INDEPENDENCE

Wapsipinicon Mill and Museum

After three years of construction, the Wapsipinicon Mill opened for business in Independence in 1870 when Iowa's primary crop was wheat. The six-story mill, one of the largest in the state, updated its machinery as time went on, from water-powered equipment to equipment powered by electricity the mill generated. The crops it ground also changed to oats, corn, rye and soybeans, which all became feed for farm animals.

The mill, made of stone, brick and timbers, operated until 1976, when it was turned over to the Buchanan County Historical Society to become the Wapsipinicon Mill and Museum. Displays in the mill relate to when it was in use during the 1870s and how it was a part of the agriculture industry. Visitors can see equipment used in the mill then, including storage bins for grain, milling machines, millstones and more, such as belt and bucket elevators that moved grains between places in the mill.

The mill is open from mid-May to mid-October.

LIME SPRINGS

Hayden Prairie State Preserve

A rare rusty-patched bee approaches a flower at Hayden Prairie, one of the very few remaining areas of native prairie in the state.

When European Americans arrived in this part of the Midwest, more than 28 million acres of tall-grass prairie covered up to 85 percent of what would become Iowa. A mere 70 years passed between the white settlers' arrival in the 1830s and the disappearance of the tall-grass prairie. Now, less than a tenth of 1 percent of that prairie endures. At 242 acres, Hayden Prairie, about 5 miles west of Lime Springs, is the largest remnant outside of the Loess Hills in western Iowa. (That 3,000-acre preserve, called Broken Kettle Grasslands, is owned by the Nature Conservancy, which maintains a buffalo herd there, and is not open to the public.)

Surveys here have counted more than 46 kinds of grasslands birds, 20 butterfly species and more than 200 types of plants, including at least 100 varieties of wildflowers. Grasses that grow higher than 5 feet may have 15-foot-long roots.

Although this land had been grazed by livestock and mown for hay before the state acquired it in 1945, it was never plowed.

Lidtke Mill

Built as a sawmill in 1857, Lidtke Mill is the last of thirteen mills powered by the Upper Iowa River. In just a few years, builder Melvin Marsh also began grinding wheat as the demand for flour grew. The mill went through a succession of owners who had good times and bad as crops flourished and failed over the next several years. After it burned down in 1894, James Stafford built a new mill on the site to grind corn into animal feed. He also installed a turbine to produce electricity for the community of Lime Springs.

When D.W. Davis bought the mill in 1915, he added a new dynamo so it could also provide electricity to Chester, another nearby community. In 1917, he acquired French buhr stones that had been imported in the 1850s by former governor William Larrabee to make finer flour at his Clermont mill. Davis's son-in-law Herman Lidtke took over the mill in 1918 and ran it until closing it forever in 1960.

Today, the mill is much as it was when Lidtke locked the door and walked away. The milling equipment and electrical generators and switching equipment are still in place, making this one of the few mills with intact machinery from when it was in use.

Lidtke Mill is open on Saturday and Sunday afternoons in the summer.

MARQUETTE

Effigy Mounds National Monument

Before Europeans arrived in North America, its indigenous people handled their dead in many ways. Bodies were placed on platforms in trees, taken deep into caves, cremated, set adrift in canoes, placed in pits and left in the open. They were buried singly or in groups.

A bird-shaped mound is one of the animal effigies at Effigy Mounds National Monument. Researchers believe the mound builders were here from AD 620 to 1270.

For about seven centuries, the people who lived in northeast Iowa were part of a civilization called the Effigy Moundbuilders, which ranged from here to the shores of southern Lake Michigan. From about AD 620 to 1270, many members of this culture created conical mounds in which to bury their dead. They also fashioned mounds believed to be used for ceremonial or religious purposes in the shapes—called effigies—of animals. Those living toward Lake Michigan favored mounds shaped like turtles and panthers.

The people living in northeast Iowa made effigies of bears lying on their sides and birds with crescent wings.

Today, 206 mounds are known to exist within the boundaries of Effigy Mounds National Monument north of Marquette. Most are earthen domes that were used for burials and measure two to six feet high and up to twenty feet across. A few slender ridges, called linear mounds, are up to one hundred feet long. Others are compound mounds, a mix of conical and linear shapes. The linear and compound mounds are also burial mounds.

Thirty-one mounds in the national monument are effigies that are believed to be burial and ceremonial mounds. The largest, called the great bear, is 137 feet long. One of the bird effigies is 212 feet across.

Bodies were prepared for burial in four ways. Remains of one or more individuals were placed in the elements, and when the flesh was gone, their bones were gathered as one and put into a shallow pit before being covered with earth. Bodies were burned before being covered. Some were arranged in sitting positions, then buried. Others were laid flat and covered.

Researchers estimate that tens of thousands of mounds existed in North America at one time. Now, 95 percent of them have been erased by the agricultural practices of the European Americans as they moved across the continent. The ones at Effigy Mounds were probably easy to see when whites arrived, as the terrain was mostly grasslands spotted with oaks. With the advance of European-based cultures, the wildfires that once kept the prairie free of trees diminished, and they took over the prairie. Locating the mounds became hard. Now, the National Park Service manages the land so visitors can see many of the mounds here.

Although no one is sure about the mounds' history or purpose, the visitor center explains what is known and displays artifacts associated with them. The visitor center sits between two major groups of mounds.

The north unit, accessible by hiking a switchback trail that ascends the bluffs overlooking the Mississippi River, has mostly conical mounds plus four effigies, including the great bear mound.

The south unit, which has its own parking area about half a mile south of the visitor center, has most of the monument's bear mounds and all four of its bird mounds. Ten bear mounds, arranged head to tail, are called the marching bears. The distance from the trailhead of the south unit to the marching bears is about two miles, or about a one-hour hike with a five-hundred-foot gain in altitude.

NASHUA

Little Brown Church in the Vale

Usually, songs are written about an established place. The opposite is true of a country church just east of Nashua where the song came first. By the mid-1850s, Bradford was well established on the plains of Iowa. Settlers had arrived in 1844, and just twelve years later, about five hundred people lived here. The seat of Chickasaw County, it was a stop on a stagecoach line. William Pitts, a young music teacher from Wisconsin, was on a stagecoach when it paused here in 1857. Pitts, on his way to visit his fiancée in another town, took a stroll during the stop and was impressed by the beauty of a piece of land he thought would be an ideal setting for a church. Back in Wisconsin, he penned a poem he titled "Church in the Wildwood" and soon afterward set it to music.

Then he put it all aside.

In 1862, Pitts and his wife moved back to the area to be near her parents and so he could teach at the Bradford Academy. To their surprise, a church was being built where he had envisioned it.

Without knowing of Pitts's song, members of the Puritan-Congregational Church were building a church after having no permanent place to worship since being founded in 1855. They had met in various places such as homes and businesses. Soon some land was donated to them, and they went to work on the church, laying down a limestone foundation in 1860 and using lumber donated by a member. To protect the wood from the weather, they knew it had to be painted. The only color available, however, was brown. Some say it was the least expensive paint.

Pitts retrieved his song, shared it with the congregation and had his students sing it for the first time at the church's dedication in December 1864.

The next year, needing money to attend medical college, Pitts sold the rights to the song to Chicago publisher H.M. Higgins for twenty-five dollars. After earning his medical degree, Pitts practiced medicine in nearby Fredericksburg, Iowa, until he retired in 1906.

When a rail line was built to nearby Nashua, making it the area's economic hub, Bradford fell on hard times. The county seat was shifted to New Hampton. In 1888, the congregation abandoned the church, although it continued to be used for some services. By 1900, Bradford was practically out of existence.

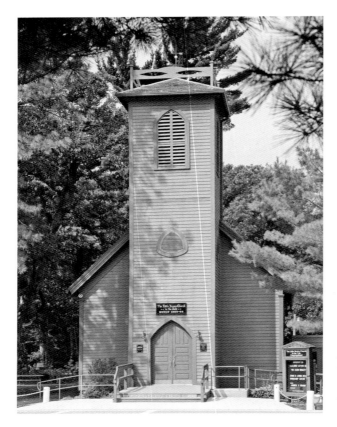

Normally songs are written about places, but in this case, the Little Brown Church, at Nashua, was built years after the song was written.

The song, however, lived on. In 1893, evangelists Arthur Chapman and Charles Alexander popularized it while traveling around the world. It really took off around 1910, when four brothers from another nearby community used it as their theme song. The foursome, known as the Weatherwax Brothers Quartet, performed for crowds as large as twenty-three thousand people at a time during their career, which lasted until the 1930s. The song is also known as "The Little Brown Church in the Vale."

As the song became popular, so did the church, and in the early part of the twentieth century, efforts were begun to restore it and its neglected property. In 1914, regular services began again. So did weddings—lots of weddings. Since records began at the church, more than 72,000 couples, including U.S. Senator Charles Grassley and his bride, Barbara, have said "I do" here. About four hundred weddings a year are performed in the church, which seats 150 on its original pews made of walnut and pine. The brass lamps are also original, as is the pump organ.

The church's congregation is about one hundred now. Nearly sixty thousand people visit it each year.

Next to the Little Brown Church is Old Bradford Pioneer Village, a collection of the county's historical buildings, including Dr. Pitts's medical office.

NEW ALBIN

Fish Farm Mounds

Similar in appearance to the conical mounds at Effigy Mounds National Monument, the thirty burial mounds located across three areas at Fish Farm Mounds are far easier to access. Just a few steps lead from a parking area to a low plateau containing the mounds. Archaeologists estimate these mounds were built between 100 BC and AD 650. The site, which is three and a half miles south of New Albin or seven and a half miles north of Lansing, offers no information. Its name comes from the family that once farmed here.

Light from the dawn sun races across prehistoric burial mounds at Fish Farm Mounds State Preserve near New Albin.

QUASQUETON

Cedar Rock State Park

When Des Moines businessman Lowell Walter, who made his fortune by inventing a way to surface country roads with asphalt, wanted a summer home for himself and his wife, Agnes, he wrote a single-spaced, one-page typewritten letter to ask architect Frank Lloyd Wright to design it. In reply, Wright wrote simply, "My dear Mr. Walter. We will design a dwelling for you. Send further details. There will be no basement nor attic."

The one-story house, called Cedar Rock, sits on forested hill west of Quasqueton and overlooks a bend in the Wapsipinicon River. The house is one of Wright's most complete designs. Besides designing its appearance, he had a hand in practically all else there. He chose the carpeting and drapes, designed the furniture, had colorful glass ornaments made as accents and selected a combination bathtub-toilet-sink for each bathroom. The dining table is segmented. Three people can sit at one segment, or all its pieces can be assembled to seat twelve.

The 150-foot-long house has two major components. One holds three bedrooms, and the other contains the living and dining rooms. Lighting in the latter comes through floor-to-ceiling windows and doors. Skylights and clerestory windows that are part of the living-dining room's raised ceiling provide more lighting. After dark, lights in coves deliver a soft glow.

Wright did not like garages because he believed they invited clutter, but the Lowells wanted to protect their cars from the weather. So Wright acquiesced by designing a carport that separates the main part of the house from the maid's quarters.

A boathouse at the river is a miniature version of the main house. It has a bedroom, kitchen and bath upstairs, and the area below is where the Walters' wooden Thompson runabout is stored. An electric winch and dolly moved it in and out of the river.

Of all the buildings Frank Lloyd Wright designed, he "signed" only twenty-five with special-fired red tiles bearing his initials to mark that these, including Cedar Rock, were his best.

Wright had started designing what he called Usonian houses in the 1930s, and Cedar Rock is one of sixty such structures. Made of brick, wood, glass and concrete, they were simple to build and maintain. Ornamentation was minimal. Their roofs were long, low and flat with large overhangs. Some say these elements influenced what would later be called ranch homes.

The house and grounds were donated in the early 1980s by the Walters to the Iowa Conservation Commission, which is now the Iowa Department of Natural Resources. Of the buildings that Wright designed, he "signed" twenty-five that he thought were his best designs with special red tiles bearing his initials. Cedar Rock is one of those twenty-five, and it's the only one in Iowa with a red tile. Eight other houses designed by Wright, along with a hotel-bank complex, are in Iowa. The hotel-bank complex and a house in Mason City (see chapter 6) are also open to the public.

SPILLVILLE

Bily Clocks Museum

Some farmers turn to hobbies when they have spare time. Brothers Joseph and Frank Bily took to carving clocks from wood on the family farm a few miles north of Spillville, which is about a dozen miles south of Decorah. Their interest in carving began after they had installed the clock mechanism in the housing that a neighbor carved for a clock. They began carving in 1913 when Joseph was thirty-three and Frank twenty-nine and used patterns to which they added their own touches. Soon, they began creating their own projects. Joseph did the designing, and Frank was the lead carver. Other than one time when Joseph carved the teeth and gears to make an all-wood clock, he and Frank used mechanisms for the clocks and their music boxes.

They called the first clock they designed and crafted with carvings of Adam and Eve, the "Creation Clock." Their second effort, called the "Hall Clock," plays jazz tunes.

In 1922, they finished their "Apostles Parade Clock," which is nine feet, ten inches tall, and took eight months to build. Every hour, chimes announce a procession of the Apostles, who emerge when a door opens.

Many clocks have moving parts. In addition to intricate carvings of a steamship, horse-drawn stagecoach, motorcycle, car, plane and balloon, the "History of Travel Clock" features a parade of musicians that drum and

A closeup of one of the clocks carved by brothers Joseph and Frank Bily of Spillville shows the elaborate carvings they made. They turned down a $1 million offer from Henry Ford in 1928 to buy one of their clocks.

march in and out of a hall to a melodious tune. Musicians abound in the clocks, such as one where a piano player with moving arms leads others playing a violin, bass and trombone. On another clock, doors pop open, and a drummer, trumpeter and tuba player step into view. Cuckoo birds dart into the open, sing their songs and then disappear in a wink.

A wedding party of four appears from behind the Little Brown Church music box and marches inside as the front doors open for them. The "American Pioneer History Clock," which is eight feet tall and weighs more than five hundred pounds, so impressed auto legend Henry Ford with its scenes of American history—which include the Pilgrims, pioneers, Lewis and Clark, an immigrant opening a door to welcome others, Christopher Columbus and Native Americans—that he came to the Bily farm to offer them $1 million for it in 1928 ($14.5 million in today's money), but they turned him down.

They wanted to keep their collection whole and never sold a clock. Instead, they kept the growing collection on their farm and charged people to see them, a dime each. The money they raised went toward the care of an older brother with physical and mental disabilities who liked clocks and their younger sister Anna, who cared for him. The brothers used only hand tools, which are displayed here, and a foot-powered sewing machine that they had converted into a jigsaw to cut the scrollwork for several clocks.

After the older brother died in 1932 and Anna passed away in 1943, Joseph and Frank saw no purpose to their collection anymore. When a Spillville resident saw them beginning to burn scraps of wood and wooden statues and learned the brothers were going to destroy the clocks, he convinced them to think about donating the clocks to the city. In 1946, they bought a two-story brick and stone building—it had had a tinsmith shop on the lower floor and a rooming house on the second—near the center of Spillville and moved the collection of clocks in there the next year.

By the time the Bily brothers set aside their chisels, hammers and homemade jigsaw in 1958, they had used about a dozen types of wood—mainly black walnut, maple, butternut and white oak that grew on their farm—to create forty clocks and two music boxes. They used only homemade glue—no screws or nails. They did not use stains either but varnish they rubbed to a shine.

Dvorak Room

Years before the Bily brothers moved their collection into town, the rooming house in that building's upstairs was the home of Czech composer Antonin Dvorak (1841–1904) and his family for one summer in the 1890s. That stay influenced some of his music. Dvorak had been hired in 1892 to teach at the National Conservatory of Music of America in New York City for three years. Accompanying him and his family was a young American who had been studying music in Prague, Joseph Kovarik. Dvorak had asked Kovarik to serve as his secretary in the United States, and Kovarik, wanting to see his homeland, said yes.

When the next spring came around, Dvorak wanted to retreat from the big city for the summer and thought about vacationing in a country home he had in Bohemia. However, after listening to Kovarik talk about where he had grown up in northeast Iowa, he said he'd like to visit Kovarik's hometown Czech community—Spillville. On June 5, Dvorak, his wife, their six children, his wife's sister and a maid arrived Spillville and set up house on the second floor of the stone-brick building. Not liking a piano made available for him, he took to using a reed organ in a neighboring house.

Within three days, Dvorak completed the first movement of his new piece for strings, a quartet, in F major, Opus 96, and was finished with the last movement on June 19. Dvorak, with Kovarik and his father and sister to round out a quartet, played the new work, which he titled the "Spillville Quartet."

Dvorak replicated horses' hoofbeats as they changed gaits in his compositions. Similarly, he integrated the sounds of daytime and how they died away when night comes. He even used the trill of a tanager, a bird not seen in his home country.

Every morning, Dvorak explored the countryside and took long walks along the Turkey River. During one stroll, he was accidentally surprised by a young woman bathing nude in the river. A "water nymph" he called her and spun the encounter into his 1900 opera *Rusalka*, a tale about an immortal water spirit of Slavic mythology who gives up her immortality for the love of a mortal prince who has been visiting the lake where she lives. Despite its being a tragic tale, it's considered to be one of the Czech language's best operas.

For ninety-three days, Dvorak enjoyed the hospitality of Spillville with its beer, kolaches, polkas and Czech companionship as he finished his quartet and a quintet, too. He took inspiration from his stay in Spillville for his later "Humoresques." He also put the finishing touches on his "New World Symphony," which made its debut in New York's Carnegie Hall in December 1893.

After "Spillville Quartet" premiered in Boston in 1894, someone gave it the nickname "American Quartet," and it stuck.

A clock the Bily brothers made in Dvorak's honor is on the main floor with their other clocks.

Inwood Ballroom

Opening with a dance in May 1922, the Inwood Ballroom is one of the last of the old-time ballrooms standing in Iowa. Open seasonally, the ballroom is the state's longest continually operating ballroom. When it opened, it featured a dining hall in a long building. In 1925, a ten-sided pavilion addition was built, and the dances were shifted into there. A stage and booths flank the dance floor, which was originally yellow pine before being replaced in 1985 by maple.

The ballroom has hosted entertainers from Glenn Miller to the Byrds to Commander Cody, covering the genres from big band to polka and rock. The venue is popular for other events including weddings.

St. Wenceslaus Church

St. Wenceslaus Church, where Dvorak played the organ during his visit, was built in 1860 and is the nation's oldest Czech Catholic church. At least two hundred unique cast-iron cruciform grave markers stand in its cemetery.

WAVERLY

Waverly Sale Barn

Twice a year, the Waverly Sale Barn holds the world's biggest horse auction in two ways. It's the largest auction of the largest horses, commonly called draft, or draught, horses.

Adult horses weigh between 1,400 and 2,000 pounds and stand up to sixty-four inches high at their shoulders. Despite their heft, they are gentle and graceful. Those with long hair on their feet look like they're flying when running. The genesis of all the draft horses in the United States came from Europe. Over the centuries, they have carried knights in their heavy shining armor, pulled farm equipment and fire engines, dragged logging sleds, pulled cannon for armies and cleared fields of rock and timber.

In the early part of the twentieth century, motorized tractors began supplying the muscle needed for farm work, and the future of the draft horses appeared dim. Then, the United States sent a million draft horses to its European allies in World War I. In 1920, just ninety-five thousand draft horses were left in the United States, and the numbers continued to plunge. In 1945, there were only two thousand.

When Arnold Hexom started the Waverly Sales in March 1948, no one was sure many draft horses would be left in a few years.

However, the numbers rebounded until peaking in the late 1970s. Allowing for variances because some owners, such as Amish farmers, do not register their horses, it's estimated that between 250,000 and 500,000 draft horses now are in the United States.

The main action during the sales in Waverly takes place the sale arena where the horses are bought and sold. Those in attendance come mostly from the United States, but some travel from as far away as the Middle East and Japan. An Amish farmer might outbid Disney for a Percheron. A Pennsylvania breeder may watch intently as the bids rise for a Belgian she's raised. As soon as a horse is led out of the showring, another's ridden in to be paraded around for everyone to see. The action is as nonstop as the auctioneer's chatter. The horses sell for thousands of dollars. In a recent year, a set of four-year-old Percherons sold for $13,500 each, and a six-year-old Belgian mare went for $9,500.

Open to the public, no one has to bid on anything to attend this event, which is like stepping back to when draft horses were the horsepower of the nation. Besides horses, auctioneers move horse-drawn machinery, trailers, harnesses, saddles, farm wagons, buggies and just about anything associated with horses.

Waverly Horse Sales holds its four-day auctions the last full week of March and the first full week of October every year. It has a very strict policy of not allowing dogs on the grounds.

AMISH

Many Amish live in Allamakee, Buchanan, Chickasaw, Clayton, Howard and Winneshiek Counties. Diamond-shaped traffic signs depicting an Amish buggy warn drivers that they can expect to come upon slow-moving horse-drawn carriages and wagons on the roads and highways in this area. Most Amish shun many aspects of modern life, yet some have stores where they sell their homemade foods, handmade quilts and handcrafted furniture. Travelers should respect the Amish way of life, which includes their desire to not be photographed.

8

EAST IOWA

ANAMOSA

Anamosa State Penitentiary Museum

Immediately outside the twenty-four-foot-tall limestone walls of the Anamosa State Penitentiary, which has about 950 male inmates and 360 staff, is something most prisons do not have—a museum. Made of stone like the prison, the museum is in a two-story building that had been a barn and was where cheese was made years ago. The museum tells the narrative of Iowa's second penitentiary, which was built by prisoners beginning in 1872. Construction went on for sixty-five years which explains why items in the museum include hammers, chisels, files and even a detonator because they were needed to quarry and shape the huge cream-colored stones to build the prison.

Also displayed are items that prisoners were not to have—such as keys and spoons made from hard plastic cups, knives shaped from sticks and other confiscated weapons. A replica of an early cell measures just four by seven feet. Its iron door was designed to weigh so much that no one person could lift it off its hinges. Other items from the past include nightsticks and overly heavy leg irons and handcuffs. Displays cover life for the inmates and the guards, and some are about the more notorious inmates, including John Wayne Gacy, who served only eighteen months of a ten-year sentence for sodomy. Later, he became notorious for his serial killings of thirty-three men and boys in Cook County, Illinois, and was executed in that state in 1994.

The administration building at the Anamosa State Penitentiary was made, like the rest of the prison, by inmates. A rare prison museum is open to the public just outside the prison walls.

Architect L.W. Forster designed the prison in the style of an Italianate castle. Unlike many other structures that are faced with limestone, the perimeter walls and the prison's major buildings are solid limestone except for materials used on their interiors.

DUBUQUE

Fenelon Place Elevator

Looking at a flat map of Dubuque, one might think Julius K. Graves lived two and a half blocks from where he worked as a banker in 1882. However, his house was on a bluff overlooking the lower portion of the city where his bank was 189 feet below. Graves, a former mayor and state senator, needed thirty minutes to ride a circuitous route between the two places in his horse-drawn carriage.

Having seen inclined railways in Europe, he decided to build a similar one here for himself. When it was completed in June 1882, a stream-driven engine attached to a winch used a rope to raise and lower his elevator car on a set of rails. Graves's gardener would let him down the seventy-four-degree rails in the morning, raise and then lower him at lunch and finally bring him up at the end of the business day. Occasionally, Graves gave his neighbors rides.

The elevator burned in 1884, and Graves rebuilt it, this time to serve the public at five cents a ride. In 1893, another fire destroyed that elevator, and ten neighbors formed the Fenelon Place Elevator Company to create a newer system using triple tracks, metal cables and two funicular cars. As one car descended the 296-foot-long tracks, the other would ascend from a shed below at the same time. Approaching each other in the middle of the slope, they would come to where the three rails broadened to four so each could pass alongside the other. The system was upgraded in 1977.

The cars, made of metal, wood and plexiglass, have no doors on their upper sides. However, the doors on their lower sides open automatically

The view atop the Fenelon Place Elevator provides a wonderful panorama of Iowa, Wisconsin and Illinois.

only when they're safely in the small building at the lower end of the line. Passengers sit on benches inside the cars during the three-minute rides.

The cars originate at the west end of Fourth Street in lower Dubuque. At the upper end, called Fenelon Place, two viewing platforms provide panoramic views of the lower portion of the city and parts of Wisconsin, Illinois and the Mississippi River. The elevator is one of Dubuque's most popular attractions and is one of the shortest and steepest railways in the world.

Julien Dubuque Monument

Born in Quebec in 1762, Julien Dubuque eventually traveled west. In his early twenties, he clerked at Michilimackinac, an outpost at the northern tip of Michigan's lower peninsula. He then joined his brother Augustin, a trader, in 1783 in what is now Prairie du Chien, Wisconsin. During his time there, he befriended the Meskwaki who lived in the area, and they eventually granted him permission in 1788 to mine for lead on their property on the Mississippi River's west side. He was the first European American they trusted with the locations of their mines and the first European American to live in Iowa.

A stone tower sits atop the grave of Julien Dubuque, the first European American to live on the west side of the Mississippi River when he started mining lead here in 1788.

At that time, the area where he lived and mined was under the control of Spain, which had purchased it from France in 1762 and held the land until 1803. In 1796, Spain gave Dubuque a land grant that was twenty-one miles long and nine miles wide on the west side of the Mississippi where he was already. Lead was an important commodity in those years. It was used in the production of pipes, pewter, paint, letters on printing presses and makeup (often with horrifying results after much use). Most of all, it was used for bullets and musket balls.

Most of Dubuque's workers were Meskwaki women. Dubuque's lead-mining operation grew into a village and then into the first city in Iowa. When Dubuque died in 1810, his Meskwaki friends buried his body in a log mausoleum on a bluff overlooking the Mississippi River. The log structure was replaced by the present limestone monument in 1897.

After his death, word of the lead mines slowly got out and lead, not gold, was responsible for one of the nation's first mineral rushes. Within twenty years of Dubuque's death, at least four thousand mining permits had been issued in this area.

William A. Black

The National Mississippi River Museum and Aquarium is one of the best places in Dubuque to visit—full of displays, interactive exhibits, animals of the wetlands and fishes of the river. Among all that is the *William A. Black*, one of the last steam-powered dredges the U.S. Army Corps of Engineers used to deepen and clear channels for large boats and tows on the inland waterways. Some other riverboats were converted to dredges, but the *Black* was designed as a dredge from the start, and it worked primarily on the Missouri River. Overall, it looks like a passenger riverboat that snagged part of an oil derrick on the big deck at its bow. Besides clearing channels in the rivers, the *Black* removed sediments from boat harbors and supplied fill where needed on riverside construction projects.

Floating in Dubuque's Ice Harbor, a man-made bay alongside the Mississippi River, the 277-foot-long *Black* was built in West Virginia in 1934. It burned heavy oil to produce steam that would turn the boat's twenty-foot-diameter sidewheels and drive the mechanisms—supported by the derrick on the bow—that sucked up sediment at the river bottom and deposited it on shore through a long floating pipeline. Jets of water could be pumped through underwater nozzles to loosen river sediment.

Built with a steel hull and wooden superstructure, *Black* has three decks. The main deck, which also serves as the top of the hull, holds the boilers, the propulsion system, dredging equipment, a water distillation plant and a wastewater treatment system.

The second deck has fourteen staterooms for officers, a galley, pantry, six cabins, an officers' mess, crews' quarters with seventeen sets of bunks and a crews' mess. Normally, a crew of forty-nine men worked on the boat, but it could accommodate up to sixty-three.

The pilot house sits on the third deck. As with all workboats on the river, it is surrounded by glass for maximum visibility. Two smokestacks rising above the rear of the deck are hinged so they could lay down to go under low bridges.

Built when oil was thought to be endless, *William A. Black* consumed seven thousand gallons a day in normal operations. That proved to be too costly for the corps during the 1973 OPEC oil embargo, and the boat was retired.

MAQUOKETA

Hurstville Lime Kilns

Not to be confused with the limes that grows on citrus trees, lime has been made from limestone for thousands of years. As long ago as 2500 BC, it was mixed with water and aggregates, usually sand, to create mortar that adhered the stones of buildings to each other in ancient Pakistan. Egyptians used it on their pyramids.

It also was used agriculturally to reduce the acidity of soils.

When Alfred Hurst learned of the limestone deposits in this area, he built four large stone kilns in the 1870s about two miles north of Maquoketa. They would produce lime that was used mostly in the construction of buildings and bridges in this part of the Midwest.

Limestone quarried nearby was broken into pieces small enough to fit into a kiln where wood-burning fires baked it at 1,650 degrees Fahrenheit to reduce it to powder. When cooled, it was removed from the kiln, packed into barrels and shipped to where needed. To speed the lime's delivery, Hurst created a railroad to the kilns in 1888, replacing the horse-drawn wagons.

Silent since 1930, these four kilns were producing up to eight thousand barrels of lime powder a day, used to make mortar in construction.

Excepting the cold months, the business was burning up to fifty million pounds of wood a year in each kiln to produce about eight thousand barrels of lime a day.

Another process for creating mortar without using much lime was invented in the early 1800s. Called Portland cement, it was less expensive to make than the older method, but it didn't become popular for many years. However, when Portland cement did catch on, the demand for lime fell, and the kilns were slowly shut down until their fires were extinguished in 1930. The small company town named Hurstville that had been built near the kilns disappeared.

The site is now owned by the Jackson County Historical Society.

61 Drive-In Theater

Although the nation's first drive-in movie theater opened in 1933 in Camden, New Jersey, they didn't catch on until the automobile's increasing popularity after World War II changed many aspects of American culture. In the late 1950s, nearly five thousand drive-in theaters were showing movies across America. About seventy were in Iowa.

Now, only four remain—Blue Grass Drive-In near the Quad Cities, Superior 71 near Spirit Lake, Valle Drive-In (built in 1948, it's the state's oldest) in Newton and 61 Drive-In near Delmar, just south of Maquoketa.

Despite changes such as digital projection and new sound systems, the 61 Drive-In is similar to when it opened in 1950. Some people arrive hours early to pick out a favorite spot to park on the lawn in front of the large screen that looms over nearby U.S. 61. On many evenings, moviegoers spread blankets across the grass, set up chairs and visit while waiting for darkness to fall so the movies can begin. Children enjoy the swing set, and teens play volleyball. Between the movies, people crowd the concession stand, which spreads the aromas of popcorn, hot dogs, pretzels and pizza.

Some folks come for the movies, others to socialize, and then there are those who just want an evening of nostalgia.

QUAD CITIES

This region encompasses Bettendorf and Davenport, Iowa, and Moline, East Moline and Rock Island, Illinois, Yes, that's five communities, but the original Quad Cities name is used by everyone.

Buffalo Bill Cody Homestead

When William F. Cody, a legend of the American Wild West in the latter part of the nineteenth century, was born in a log cabin a few miles west of LeClaire in February 1847, Iowa was a territory on the western frontier. While the Cody family lived here, his father, Isaac, was hired by William Breckenridge to build a limestone house and other buildings, which he completed in 1847. However, Breckenridge died, and the Cody family moved onto the farm, now called the Cody Homestead, which is about six miles northwest of Princeton. (The birthplace near LeClaire was moved to Cody, Wyoming in 1933.) Each floor of the house has two rooms—two bedrooms upstairs and a kitchen and parlor on the first level. Original elements include the walnut flooring, lathe and plaster walls and, in the kitchen, a stone fireplace and wooden mantel. The house is furnished with items from the time that the Cody family lived there

In 1849, the Cody family moved into LeClaire alongside the Mississippi River, where they lived until 1853, when they migrated to Kansas. At the age of eleven, William served as a messenger on a wagon train. That began a never-ending life on the plains for him. He rode for the Pony Express. As a civilian army scout, he earned the Medal of Honor for bravery in a skirmish with Native Americans near Fort McPherson, Nebraska. He earned the nickname Buffalo Bill supplying buffalo meat for the construction crews of the Kansas Pacific Railroad.

Then author Ned Buntline (whose real name was E.Z.C. Judson) began portraying Cody as a hero of the American West in his novels and plays, and Cody's fame spread. Cody performed in theatrical productions about the West and, in 1883, started his Buffalo Bill's Wild West Show, which cemented his role in American legends. Cody died at age seventy in Denver in 1917 and was buried at the base of nearby Lookout Mountain.

Buffalo Bill Museum

William F. Cody may be the namesake for the Buffalo Bill Cody Museum in LeClaire, but its real attraction is *Lone Star*, the last wood-hulled steamboat to work on the Mississippi River. Built in 1868 in what is today Clinton, Iowa, *Lone Star* started as a packet boat carrying passengers, freight and mail on regularly scheduled routes mostly on the Mississippi. The lower deck contained the boilers and engines while the upper deck held quarters for the crew. Atop it all was the glass-surrounded pilot house with its huge wooden steering wheel.

Initially, it was a sidewheeler that burned wood to provide steam to drive its engines. In 1890, *Lone Star* was converted into a sternwheeler, which increased it length to ninety feet. The boat then began anew as a towboat. Nine years later, *Lone Star* became a coal burner. In 1922, it was reconfigured once more, this time as a dredge. In the end, it was hardly anywhere near the modern age. Instead of using radio and radar like almost all other large boats on the river, *Lone Star*'s main ways of communicating were with bells, whistles and yells.

Throughout its life, *Lone Star* used river water in its boilers, and that meant shutting down the boilers, draining them and rinsing them clean every two weeks and more often when the river was muddy. At the same time, ashes in the fireboxes were swept into the river. (This was before the EPA existed.) After *Lone Star* was retired in 1968, it sat outside the museum until a glass-and-steel addition was built for it in 2008.

The museum has several other displays, including, of course, those about Buffalo Bill Cody. A re-creation of a 1920s one-room school was built in an addition to the museum, which also has displays about the works of engineer James Eads, who lived in LeClaire at one time. He was responsible for designing the first bridge to cross the Mississippi at St. Louis, an early type of diving bell to salvage material on the bottom of the river and ironclad gunboats the Union used in the Civil War. Another LeClaire resident, James J. Ryan II, invented the first automatic retractable seat belt, the collapsible steering column and, perhaps most important of all, the flight data recorder, the so-called black box found in many aircraft. An example of an early black box, painted yellow and shaped like a sphere, is at the museum.

Lagomarcino's

It's been more than a century since Italian immigrant Angelo Lagomarcino opened a confectionery store in the Quad Cities and later began making ice cream in the 1930s. To say the store is popular would be an understatement. Among its creamy and cold concoctions are ice cream sodas, sundaes, egg cremes and banana splits. The deli offers homemade sandwiches and salads. After operating only in Rock Island, Lagomarcino's opened a second location in the village of Davenport, a historic district of housing, shops and entertainment businesses. Many of its buildings were constructed in the years soon after the Civil War.

Lock and Dam 15

The Mississippi River is not like some other rivers with waterfalls and long stretches of rocky rapids that make navigation by boats impossible. Still, it drops 420 feet between its northern port for commercial shipping at St. Paul, Minnesota, and, 630 miles to the south, St. Louis, Missouri. For many years, rapids near Keokuk and Davenport, Iowa, deterred boats from trying to pass through them. In the 1930s, Congress approved the construction of twenty-seven locks and dams between the two cities to facilitate the passage of boats up and down the river. Ten of the locks and dams are alongside Iowa.

Lock and Dam 15 at Rock Island, Illinois, which is opposite Davenport, is the only lock and dam with a visitor center. It's accessed through the Moline gate of the Rock Island Arsenal with a valid photo ID. Visitors can walk along the lock as watercraft from kayaks and canoes to tows and palatial passenger riverboats move through the lock. Sightseers can also watch the lock's operations from inside the comfort of the two-story visitor center.

When any watercraft heading upstream wants to pass through the lock, its captain signals his or her intentions to the lockmaster. The lockmaster then opens the lock's lower gates, which weigh eighty-two tons each, so the boat can head into the lock. Once the boat's in the lock, the lower gates are closed. Valves are opened, allowing millions of gallons of water from the higher area of the river to flow into the lock, raising the boat up to the level of the upper river. When that's done, the upper gates are opened, and the boat moves out of the lock upstream.

The process reverses when a boat goes downriver. No pumps are used, just the weight of the water inside and outside the lock. About the fastest a boat can pass through a lock is twenty minutes.

Going through a lock for a big pack of barges and a tugboat is, however, more complicated and takes more time. Above St. Louis, many of these packs (usually called tows) consist of a tugboat—which, here, is used strictly for pushing barges, not tugging or towing them—at the rear of a set of fifteen barges arranged in three columns of five barges each. This makes an assembly that's longer than the lock and means a tow has to be split into two units to transit the lock.

To do this, a towboat pushes the entire tow into the lock, where its crew separates the barges into two sections by freeing the cables connecting the front nine with the back six barges and the towboat. The first section of barges is secured in the lock by cables. When the towboat backs out of the lock with the remaining six barges, the gates are closed, and the nine barges within the lock are raised or lowered to the elevation of the next part of the river. When the gates ahead of the front section of barges are open, powerful winches pull them out of the lock into next section of the river. Those gates are then closed, and the rear section of barges and the tugboat go through the locking processing until they can be reattached to the front section of barges. A fifteen-barge tow can take up from one and a half to two and a half hours to pass through locks like the one at Rock Island, depending on how experienced the crew is.

Each barge can carry 1,500 tons of cargo, ranging from coal and grains to oil, sand and timber. A tow of 15 barges carries as much freight as a train about three miles long or 225 semi-truck trailers. Sixty percent of the nation's grain exports and 20 percent of its coal travel on the Mississippi River.

Every Saturday and Sunday during the summer, free guided tours are given out on the locks at 10:00 a.m. and 2:00 p.m. Call 309-794-5308 beforehand, as reservations are required.

Quad Cities Pizza

Just like Chicago is known for its deep-dish pizza, the Quad Cities have their Quad City–style pizza. Brothers Frank and Tony Maniscalco are credited with introducing this style of pizza in the 1950s, but now many pizzerias in the Quad Cities make variations of it. The appearance of this pizza is the most conspicuous difference from most other pizzas in that while this pizza is round, it's cut into strips—sometimes by cooking scissors—rather than the more traditional triangles.

The basic Quad City–style pizza has a crust that is thicker than thin crust pizzas, and malt and molasses are mixed into the dough. Likewise, fennel is mixed into the crumbled sausage. Cayenne pepper and flakes of red chili spice up the tomato sauce. Once all that is in place, it's buried by cheese from edge to edge and baked.

9

EAST-CENTRAL IOWA

AMANA

Amana Colonies

The Amana Colonies are a group of seven villages begun in 1855 by eight hundred Germans who had left their homeland for religious freedom. Before reaching Iowa, they stayed in western New York for about a dozen years before deciding to find more land for their growing religious movement, called the Community of True Inspiration.

After buying twenty-six thousand acres less than twenty miles northwest of Iowa City, then Iowa's capital city, they platted six villages in an L-shaped line near the Iowa River. The towns were arranged so each was two miles from another. For a while, the founders thought of calling their villages Bleibetreu, which is German for "remaining faithful," but that was dropped for the biblical word *amana*, which means the same thing. The main village was named Amana, but each of the other villages has that word in its name too—High Amana, Middle Amana, East Amana, West Amana and South Amana.

In 1859, the community chose to incorporate as a business, the Amana Society, which planned for the villages to be as self-sufficient as possible. Women, men and children had certain tasks.

No one owned property or a business. Everything was owned by the society, which provided housing, meals, schools, churches, occupations and businesses. Inspirationalists, which is what the members called themselves,

Built in 1858, the Amana General Store in High Amana, one of the seven colonies, is now part of the Amana Museum.

might have received twenty-five to fifty dollars a year, but otherwise, no one was paid a salary.

Religion was important. Everyone went to church eleven times a week. Women and children sat separately from the men. Courting age for women was twenty-one to twenty-four. Men could not marry before they were twenty-four. All were expected to marry within the community.

Each village had a post office, general store, bakery, churches, dairy, school, forty to one hundred houses and kitchens with dining halls. A village had its own gardens, orchards, vineyards, wineries, breweries and icehouses. Some had specific industries, such as Amana, with its woolen mill and furniture factory. Each village had (and still has) its own cemetery where the headstones face east, and all are the same size, aligning with the belief that all people are equal. All are buried in the order in which they died.

Even though the group of villages was to be self-sufficient, the Inspirationalists realized trade with the outside world was important because they could not provide every item they needed, and they needed to sell their goods, including crafts, foods, woolen materials, clocks, wine and printed calico clot, beyond the colonies. Because a railroad line went through the small town of Homestead, just two miles south of Amana, the society bought the entire town and made it into the seventh Amana colony.

By 1908, more than 1,800 Inspirationalists lived in the colonies, leading to change. Married couples began cooking in their homes, causing the number of community kitchens to dwindle. There had been fifty-five at one time. Some members preferred more secularism with less restrictions by the church. In 1932, the Inspirationalists voted to disband the Amana Society as a single entity, an event still called the "Great Change." It then became two organizations: the Amana Church Society, a nonprofit dealing with religious matters, and a for-profit business-only corporation that would be called the Amana Society Inc. The Amana name was given to a line of appliances that was begun in Middle Amana in the 1930s and continues in a factory complex there under the ownership of Whirlpool Corp.

More than 450 buildings from the communal years stand in the seven villages. Amana, the largest colony, has the most businesses, including restaurants known for serving family-style meals. The Woolen Mill is the only wool mill in Iowa. Near it, artisans craft furniture and clocks in the original furniture factory. Breweries and wineries make their own beverages.

In Middle Amana, Hahn Bakery converted its wood-burning oven to gas years ago but continues the traditions of making breads, pastries and sweets. The last of the bakeries in the colonies, Hahn Bakery is where work begins early every morning. Usually, the baked goods are sold out in a few hours.

The Amana Heritage Museum is the mainstay of the Amana Heritage Society. Located in a former residence in Amana, its exhibits explain the original Amana Society, and more displays are in the adjacent 1870 schoolhouse and washhouse.

The museum has four properties in other villages, and admission can be purchased for all five sites at any of the locations.

High Amana has its original 1857 General Store, which is part museum and part retailer with the original glass-and-wood display cases, wood floors and pressed-tin ceiling panels.

Homestead has its original brick church that was built in 1865. The bare wooden pews feature no artistic embellishment. The village also has an original blacksmith shop, which contains a print shop.

Middle Amana has one of the communal kitchens and a cooper shop, where barrels were made to contain the goods made in the villages. The kitchen was built in 1863 and is the last communal kitchen standing with everything once used in it still there. The dining room is similar.

Finally, some people wonder, are the Amana Amish? No, despite the similarity of the names.

CEDAR RAPIDS

Grant Wood Studio and Home

From 1924 to 1935, artist Grant Wood used the upstairs of this two-story brick garage as his studio and residence, and this is where he painted several of his famous works.

The garage was a carriage house that dates from the 1890s when the mansion next door was built for George B. Douglas, a partner in a grain mill that became Quaker Oats. John D. Turner and his son David bought the house in 1924 to change it into a funeral home. The Turners, who were patrons of Wood, hired him to redesign the mansion for their new business.

They also offered him the second floor of the carriage house free of rent in exchange for some of his paintings. This allowed Wood to quit teaching at a high school and paint full-time. He rearranged and rebuilt the new space to serve as a studio and home for himself, his sister Nan Wood Graham and their mother, Hattie. As a carriage house, the building had no address, so Wood gave it one: 5 Turner Alley.

He designed its galley-style kitchen and bathroom as small as practical to leave a large open area for his studio. Two rollaway beds could be pulled into the open from below storage cupboards, and his tools and paintings were hidden on a moveable wall. Wood installed a large window and built the belfry to allow more light into the largest area of the studio-home. Flowers, artifacts, small pieces of art and the telephone occupied niches he built into the walls.

Besides *American Gothic*, Wood painted other well-known pieces here, including *Stone City, The Appraisal, The Midnight Ride of Paul Revere* and *Daughters of the American Revolution*.

Above: Originally the upper story of a mortuary's garage in Cedar Rapids, this space became Grant Wood's studio and home for some years, including when he painted *American Gothic*.

Left: One of Grant Wood's early projects was the creation of this stained-glass window in the Cedar Rapids' Veterans Memorial.

In 1935, Wood accepted a position at the University of Iowa, and he left Cedar Rapids to live in Iowa City. He died in 1942 and is buried in Anamosa.

In 1972, David Turner's son and daughter-in-law, John B. Turner II and Happy Turner, donated eighty-four of Wood's artworks to the Cedar Rapids Museum of Art, which has the largest collection of Wood's art.

While in Cedar Rapids, those interested in Wood's art should visit the Veteran's Memorial, where he designed and built a stained-glass window honoring those who fought in World War I.

IOWA CITY

Devonian Fossil Gorge

Two floods washed over the spillway of the Coralville Dam in 1993 and 2008, scouring the bottom of the Iowa River and its banks and uncovering countless fossils from the Devonian age, which was about 365 million years ago. That's nearly 200 million years before dinosaurs lived. At that time, a warm shallow sea, estimated to be eight to fifteen feet deep, covered much of what would become the Midwest and dying animals and plants settled to the bottom of it. Over millions of years, they became fossilized corals, brachiopods, crinoids, sponges, bryozoans and trilobites.

Visitors can walk through the gorge and handle the fossils, but collecting is not allowed and earns a $500 fine. The gorge is part of a park administered by the U.S. Army Corps of Engineers and which has campgrounds, picnic shelters, boat ramps, beaches and twenty miles of trails.

Because floods washed out part of the waterway below the Coralville Dam, visitors can now find fossils from 375 million years ago, but law prohibits keeping them.

Old Capitol Museum

Built from 1840 to 1842 of limestone quarried nearby, the statehouse served first as the Iowa Territory's capitol. When Iowa became the twenty-ninth state in the union in 1846, the building then became the state's first capitol. In 1857, the state government moved to Des Moines to be more centrally located in the state, and the former capitol became part of the University of Iowa. Classrooms and offices occupied the building until the 1970s. Six years of renovations followed, returning the building to its appearance in 1850 and making it into a state historical museum.

More renovations followed, and a fire triggered by a contractor's torch destroyed the dome in 2001, delaying the overall renovations until May 2006, when the building was opened to the public once more

Left: Built from 1840 to 1842 to serve first as the capitol of Iowa Territory, the statehouse then became the first capitol of the new state of Iowa in 1846.

Right: An elegant spiral staircase connects the first and second floors in what is now the Old Capitol Museum in Iowa City.

The second-floor chambers of the senators and representatives appear as they were in 1850. The governor's office and supreme court are on the main floor, and an elegant reverse spiral staircase connects the two floors. The wooden Corinthian columns at the top of the staircase are part of the original construction.

The university uses the building on occasion, and it's also used for receptions, weddings and other events.

MUSCATINE

Pearl Button Museum

Although buttons have been around in one form or another for about five thousand years, German immigrant John Frederick Boepple began a new industry in Iowa when he opened the nation's first plant to make buttons from the shells of freshwater mussels. He had looked to start his business elsewhere but liked the quality of the mussels found in the Mississippi River near Muscatine. They were so dense that when a drill created a blank to be fashioned into a button, the blank was thick enough to not break like thinner shells found elsewhere. However, processing the mussels, which were harvested from the riverbed, was so slow as to make the business nearly unfeasible.

Then along came Nicholas Barry and Sons, a local plumbing and heating business. The Barrys were an inventive family, creating equipment used in fighting fires and hydraulic mining, and they looked at improving the world of making buttons. In 1904, they created the Barry Double Automatic, a machine that took the blanks made by other machines and polished, shaped and dyed them along with drilling holes through them. One of these machines could pop out twenty-two thousand pearl buttons a day.

The pearl button business in Muscatine took off and soon was soon producing 1.5 billion pearl buttons a year. The city called itself the Pearl Button Capital of the World. About a third of the labor force in the city was involved with the pearl button industry in one way or another. Many of those in the industry worked from their homes, the so-called mom-and-pop businesses. Muscatine eventually had at least forty-three pearl button factories.

As the years passed, mussels became harder to find in the Mississippi. To keep the businesses alive, mussels from the Ohio, Arkansas and Tennessee Rivers were shipped to Muscatine. Although plastic arrived in the 1920s, that alone did not cause the end of the pearl button industry. That came when wringer washing machines and dry-cleaning machines appeared. Their movements destroyed so many pearl buttons that many of the manufacturers went to making plastic buttons or folded. Some of the pearl button companies hung on through the 1950s, with the last closing in 1966. Two companies that make plastic buttons, however, remain in Muscatine: J&K Button Company and McKee Button Company.

Displays in the National Pearl Button Museum cover the history of the pearl button industry, from collecting the shells to creating button blanks to polishing those into buttons of all shapes, sizes and colors. The museum has Barry Double Automatics and videos show them in operation.

The museum is administered by the Muscatine History and Industry Center.

Pine Creek Grist Mill

Almost as soon as European Americans settled in an area in Iowa, someone would build a mill to grind the crops grown on newly plowed soil. One of the first men to live in Muscatine County, Benjamin Nye built a sawmill near the Mississippi River here in 1835, but it was destroyed in a flood. Then he built another about a mile up Pine Creek from its confluence with the Mississippi. For some reason, he did not like it, describing it was a "miserable little corn cracker."

Built in 1848, the Pine Creek Grist Mill has its original equipment. It's located in Wildcat Den State Park.

In 1848, Nye began building the one that survives today. It's the oldest operating mill standing where it was built between the Rocky Mountains and the Mississippi River.

Made of native oak that's connected by wooden pegs, the three-and-a-half-story mill first ground corn into animal feed and wheat into flour. In 1877, a steam system was installed to power the mill, and it was updated again in 1890. One of the mill's owners built a bridge across the creek so farmers could reach the mill when the water was too high for them to ford the stream.

Business took a downturn around World War I, and the mill was used less and less. In 1927, the mill became part of the 423-acre Wildcat Den State Park, and a private group interested it has put at least fifty thousand hours into restoring it to its 1890 condition.

WEST BRANCH

Herbert Hoover Birthplace

Former president Herbert Hoover was born in this two-room cottage on August 10, 1874, and later became the first president to be born west of the Mississippi River. The parents and their three children slept in one room, and the other served as a parlor, dining room and kitchen. Fabric was stuffed between the inner and outer walls as insulation.

Hoover's father, Jesse, owned the blacksmith shop across the street from the house. In 1877, the family moved into a larger house a short distance away. Raised as a Quaker, Herbert, as an adult, did not often attend meetings, although he believed in their principles throughout his life.

When Herbert was six years old, his father suffered a fatal heart attack. Three and a half years later, his mother, Hulda, died. Herbert, his older brother and younger sister then went to live with various relatives for a few years. Finally, in 1885, an uncle in Oregon took in Herbert.

Without having a high school diploma, Hoover was accepted into Stanford University, where he majored in geology. Following graduation, he worked for himself and others to develop new mines and rehabilitate old ones. His work took him to Australia, China, England and other countries. During and after World War I, he became famous for his skillful handling of relief efforts, something he repeated following the Great Mississippi Flood

Herbert Hoover was born in this small house in 1874; he was the first president born west of the Mississippi River. His father owned a nearby blacksmith shop.

of 1927. Hoover served as secretary of commerce for President Warren G. Harding. He was courted by both political parties.

In 1928, he ran as the Republican candidate for president and won forty of forty-eight states. He chose Charles Curtis, who had a Native American mother, as his vice president.

When the Great Depression hit, practically everyone blamed Hoover, and in the 1932 election, he won only six states. After World War II, he returned to working with relief efforts in Europe for President Truman and reorganized the departments in the federal executive branch.

Even though Hoover never lived in West Branch again, he took an interest in the house where he was born. After some previous tries, he and his wife, Lou, finally acquired it in 1935 and restored it to how it had been when he lived there.

Lou Hoover died in 1944. The former president died in 1964. Both are buried near the Herbert Hoover Presidential Library, a short walk from his birthplace. A functioning replica of his father's blacksmith shop is on the grounds. A restored 1857 Friends meetinghouse, built by the Society of Friends, or Quakers, is near the birthplace, too.

WILTON

Wilton Candy Kitchen

Nobody should have any question that a good time is going to be had by walking through the front door of the Wilton Candy Kitchen. "Candy Soda Lunch" announces the yellow-and-blue sign above the striped awning that shades the front windows and door trimmed in Coca-Cola red.

When Irish immigrant Robert McIntire opened his Confectionary Ice Cream Parlor Soda Fountain in this building in 1850, he probably had no idea it would still be going strong although under a different name more than 160 years later. Now, it's the nation's oldest soda fountain. When renamed as the Wilton Candy Kitchen, it truly was where all types of candy were made. Government-mandated sugar shortages during World War II put an end to the making of candy, but the ice cream and other cold treats continued—and continue to be served today.

It was here that longtime owners George and Thelma Nopoulos told a one young man who stopped in years ago why true soda fountains supply such little spoons to the visitors. "That's so they'll take longer to savor what they're eating," said George, whose father had also ran the business.

Travelers in eastern Iowa should be aware that many Amish live in Johnson and Washington Counties. Please refer to the section titled "Amish" at the end of chapter 7.

10

SOUTHEAST IOWA

BURLINGTON

Snake Alley

Those who believe Iowa is flat should visit Burlington, which sits on many hills and valleys. For many years after Burlington was founded in 1833, one particular hill blocked wheeled carts, coaches and wagons from traveling between the downtown area at the base of the hill and a residential area at the top. Putting in a straight street was out of the question. On a map, Washington Street, at the base of the hill, was 275 feet south of Columbia Street. In reality, Columbia was about 60 feet higher than Washington.

Snake Alley in Burlington is often described as "the crookedest" street in the nation. Its curves have allowed vehicles to traverse a steep slope since it was built in 1894.

Horses could not pull anything up the steep slope, and taking a wagon down would be tempting fate.

Then German immigrant Charles Starker and his American-born son Arthur thought of the back-and-forth roads they had seen on the hills in Germany. Teaming up with William Stregh, an engineer and architect, and George Kriechbaum, who made paving bricks, they designed a series of two quarter and five half curves to run between Washington and Columbia Streets. When the project was completed in 1894, it was regarded as part of North Sixth Street although several locals nicknamed it Snake Alley, and the name stuck. Some people also call it the world's crookedest street.

Made of limestone and blue clay and laid in such a way to aid horses walking up hill, Kriechbaum's bricks remain in use today.

FORT MADISON

Old Fort Madison

In May 1808, the U.S. government negotiated with the Sauk who lived in this region to build a trading post. The Sauk were receptive at first but took exception when the U.S. Army began building a fort there, too, its first outpost on the Upper Mississippi River. Considering that a provocation, the Sauk attempted to infiltrate the fort during talks with its commander, First Lieutenant Alpha Kingsley. Learning of their plot, Kingsley, standing near a cannon, convinced the Sauk to leave.

The fort was poorly sited, on the river's floodplain and below hills to the north where an enemy could shoot down into it. Allied with the British in the War of 1812, the Sauk, Fox and Winnebago attacked the fort in April 1812 and laid siege to it for four days the following September. Another siege came in July 1813.

Sometime after that siege, realizing the odds were against his troops, the new commander, First Lieutenant Thomas Hamilton, decided to abandon the fort. The men set it on fire and made their way to boats hidden along the Mississippi to successfully flee downriver. All that was left were some brick chimneys, one of which still stands.

Because of how the city of Fort Madison has grown over the years, building a re-creation of the fort on its original site was impossible. So, a

A reenactor prepares to fire his rifle at Old Fort Madison, a re-creation of the fort that was here during the War of 1812.

replica, called Old Fort Madison, was built about a half mile west of the original fort's site. Excepting a long extension on the north wall of the real fort, the replica is much like the original.

Reenactors are at Old Fort Madison to interpret its history for visitors.

KEOKUK

National Cemetery

During the Civil War, five hospitals in Keokuk tended to the wounded brought by steamboats from distant battlefields. (The only action in that war that directly involved Iowa was more like a skirmish in August 1861 near

The National Cemetery in Keokuk, the only one in Iowa, began in the Civil War when the city had five hospitals handling troops who arrived on riverboats from distant battlefields.

the state border just north of Athens, Missouri.) The National Cemetery in Keokuk was established in 1862 on donated land to bury those troops who died in Keokuk. More than six hundred Union soldiers are interred here, as are eight Confederate troops. The remains of additional soldiers were reinterred here when the cemeteries at Fort Yates, North Dakota, and Fort Des Moines, Iowa, were closed in the first half of the twentieth century.

At last count, about five thousand military personnel, veterans and their family members are buried here.

LOUISA COUNTY

Toolesboro Mounds State Preserve

Members of the Hopewell Culture built seven conical mounds between 200 BC and AD 100. While two can be easily visited, the rest are fenced off in the nearby woods. Up to twelve may have been here before some disappeared because of the onset of European American settlement. Some researchers believe a Native American village was here, but no evidence of it has been found. One of the two mounds that can be seen may be the largest Hopewell mound found in Iowa, measuring eighty feet in diameter and eight feet high.

Various people, some operating in the name of science, excavated the mounds in the nineteenth century, finding human remains, stone smoking pipes, stone and copper tools, shell and pearl beads and sheets of mica. Burial mounds are respectfully not explored anymore.

The group is named after a town that existed here and was platted in 1837 settled by William Toole, a merchant who was also its postmaster.

MONTROSE

Galland School

A replica of the small log structure that was Iowa's first school stands close to the Mississippi River less than four miles south of Montrose. In 1830, Isaac Galland built the ten-by-thirteen-foot schoolhouse of logs with mud packed between them and hired a teacher to conduct its classes for the three years it was open. The site is managed by Lee County Conservation Board.

VAN BUREN COUNTY

Several sites in Van Buren County have banded to call themselves the Villages of Van Buren County.

Bentonsport: Mason House

In 1846, William Robinson hired a number of Mormon men to build a hotel near the Des Moines River in Bentonsport to provide lodging for those traveling the river on steamboats. The river was then navigable to Fort Dodge, more than two hundred miles upriver. Besides bringing in goods from the east and then taking deliveries to the east, the riverboats acted like taxis, shuttling the residents of the area between the riverside communities.

Built in 1846 as an inn to accommodate travelers on the nearby Des Moines River, Mason House Inn is now a bed-and-breakfast in Bentonsport.

Built by Mormons who came from nearby Nauvoo, Illinois, Robinson's hotel was first known as Ashland House. When Lewis Mason bought the hotel in 1857, he and his wife renamed the inn Phoenix Hotel. However, the locals called it Mason House, and that name took root.

Before the Civil War, Mason House was a stop on the Underground Railroad, a series of secret routes used by slaves escaping Missouri—then a slave state—to freedom in the north. It also served as a hospital at times.

Today, Mason House Inn is a bed-and-breakfast. Six guest rooms are in the main house, two more in a former railroad depot and one in a renovated 1952 caboose once used by the Roscoe, Snyder and Pacific Railway in Texas. Many furnishings bought by the Masons in the mid-nineteenth century are still in the rooms.

Bonaparte: Bonaparte Pottery
National Historic Archaeological Site

A pottery company opened in 1865 on the banks of the Des Moines River in Bonaparte, but it burned down ten years later. Another firm,

Pottery molds from 1875, unearthed a few years ago, are still used to create stoneware at Bonaparte Pottery National Archeological Site.

Hanback and Wilson, built a new pottery at the site and was soon churning out pieces of earthenware and stoneware by the thousands as well as drainpipes, flowerpots and fireproof brick for the region. That business lasted until the early 1900s, when a lumber company took over the site and, for whatever the reason, literally buried everything related to Hanback and Wilson.

Fast-forward to 1992, when Marilyn and Donnie Thomas bought the property. A year later, the Des Moines River flooded and revealed elements of the old potteries, which the Thomases didn't know were there. With help from the University of Iowa and others, the Thomases began unearthing all types of pottery, pottery molds and even equipment such as a pug mill, which was, in its day, a horse-powered mixer of pottery clays. Because the studies revealed how significant Hanback and Wilson Pottery had been to the region, the Thomases' property was named a national historic site. It is the only pottery on its original site in Iowa.

The unearthing continues, and Marilyn Thomas estimates the remains of the old potteries are not even half uncovered. Visits are by appointment only because the site is a work in progress.

Keosauqua: Hotel Manning

When Edwin Manning held his Hotel Manning's grand opening in April 1899, it was regarded as one of the finest-looking guesthouses in southeast Iowa. Some said it had the look of a palatial steamboat, although the years of steamers on the Des Moines River were gone about thirty years by then. They had been supplanted by railroads that took passengers and freight to almost anywhere in Iowa.

Unfortunately, being so close to the river had its drawbacks. Two years later, the hotel had seven feet of water in it due to a flood. Still, the owners persisted. From the 1940s into the 1980s, Hotel Manning was mostly a boardinghouse. Then in the 1980s, its fortunes began to turn around, and its appearance improved.

Now, it operates as a boutique hotel. The lobby is the hotel's most striking space, its ornate pine woodwork giving visitors the feeling that they're in 1899. The dining room is similarly beautiful. Both rooms have sixteen-foot-high ceilings. Antiques fill the sixteen guest rooms.

Van Buren County Courthouse

Built in 1843, the Van Buren Courthouse is the oldest active courthouse in Iowa and west of the Mississippi River. Designed in the Greek Revival style of architecture, the two-story building has a framework of oak and walnut. Locally made bricks were used for the exterior walls. Originally, a square tower topped the building, and two circular wooden staircases connected the first and second floors. However, the tower and stairs were removed years ago.

Many county offices remain on the main floor, while others were transferred to a new building in 2004. The courtroom occupies the second floor, and although many court activities are now held in the new district court building, the original courtroom is used a few times a year. That maintains its status as the oldest active courthouse in Iowa.

In this courtroom in 1846, William McCauley was sentenced to be hanged for the murder of Don Ferdinand Coffman. Coffman had accused McCauley of having an "alleged improper intimacy" with his wife, and McCauley later shot and killed Coffman in August 1844. The bullet also killed Coffman's infant daughter, who he was carrying in his arms.

A gallows was erected in a natural amphitheater near the courthouse, and on April 4, McCauley was hanged, the only person to be executed in Van Buren County. Afterward, the area was called Hangman's Hollow.

MANY AMISH LIVE IN southeastern Iowa, and travelers should exercise caution when they see diamond-shaped traffic signs depicting an Amish buggy. See "Amish" at the end of chapter 7.

ABOUT THE AUTHOR

Mike Whye grew up traveling as a member of a military family that, every few years, moved to another U.S. Air Force base within the states. His parents treated each new posting as an opportunity to learn about that area, such as the history-rich states of New England, the shores of the southeastern states and the Midwest from the Canadian border down into deep Texas.

The family explored much more than close to where they lived. They went on cross-country journeys that Mike continued into his college years and beyond. Eventually, he ended up traveling through all forty-eight lower states.

He began writing articles and supplying photographs for them while in college. After earning degrees at the University of Nebraska at Lincoln and Iowa State University, he worked with a newspaper in Omaha, Nebraska, and then directed the public relations of a 150-person engineering-architecture firm in northwest Iowa. In 1983, he left the firm to become a full-time freelance writer-photographer, working primarily with travel and general interest magazines and newspapers.

His stories and photos have appeared in the *Omaha World-Herald*, the *Des Moines Register*, *Air & Space*, *AAA Home & Away*, *AAA World*, *Persimmon Hill*, *The Iowan* and *Nebraska Life*, plus books published by National

Geographic, Readers Digest, Children's Press, Meredith Publications and Walking Stick Press.

Mike has also photographed architecturally significant structures for a division of the National Park Service and has supplied text and photos for the Nebraska Tourism Commission and the Iowa Tourism Office. In 2004, Mike was presented with the Friend of Iowa Tourism Award by the Iowa Economic Development Authority for the stories and photos he has produced about Iowa over the years in newspapers and magazines.

A member of Midwest Travel Journalists Association (formerly Midwest Travel Writers Association) since 1989, Mike served as its president from 2000 to 2004 and has served in other positions as well.

Mike lives in Council Bluffs with his wife, Dorie Stone.